Dream Catcher Adult Coloring Book

This Coloring book belongs to:

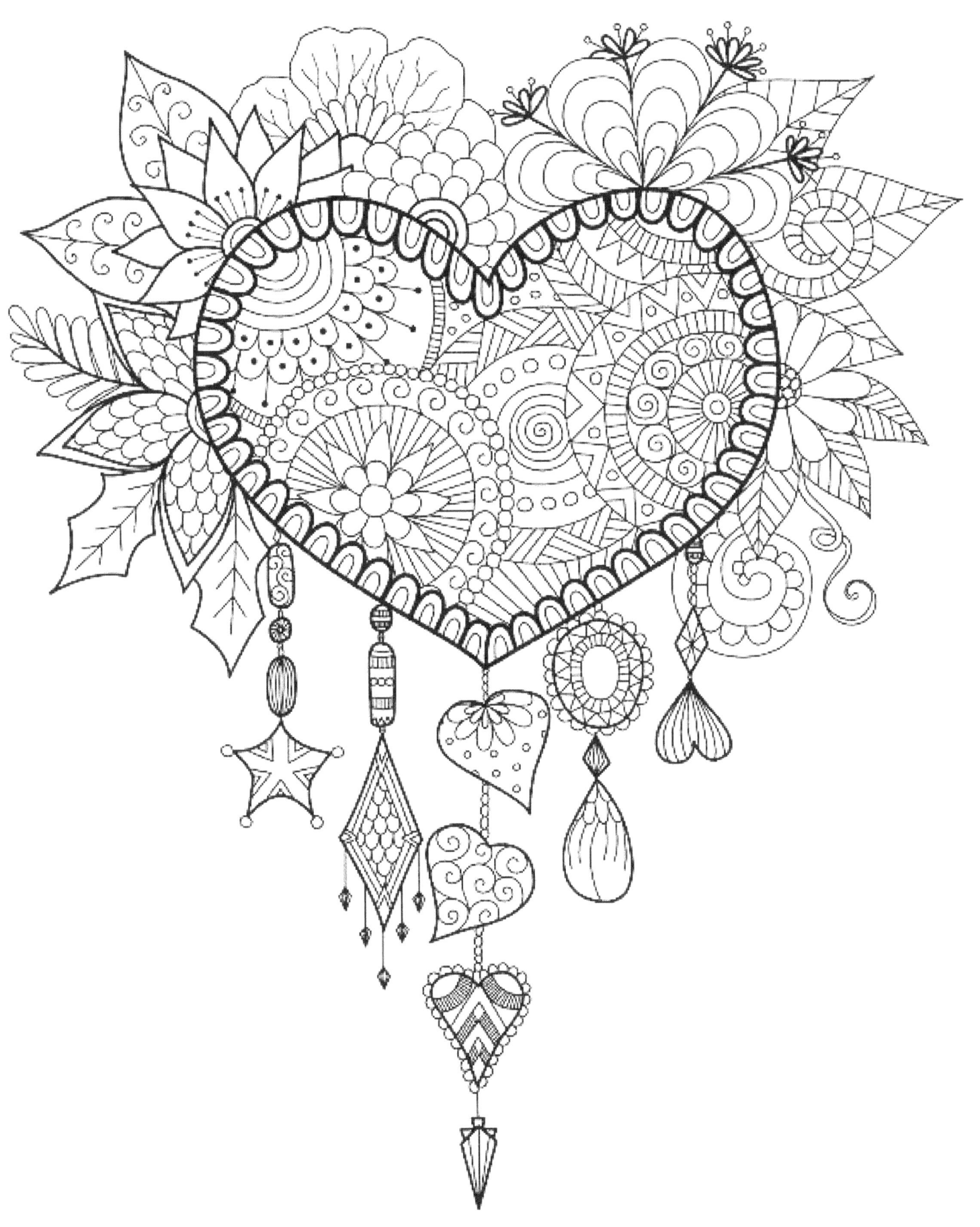

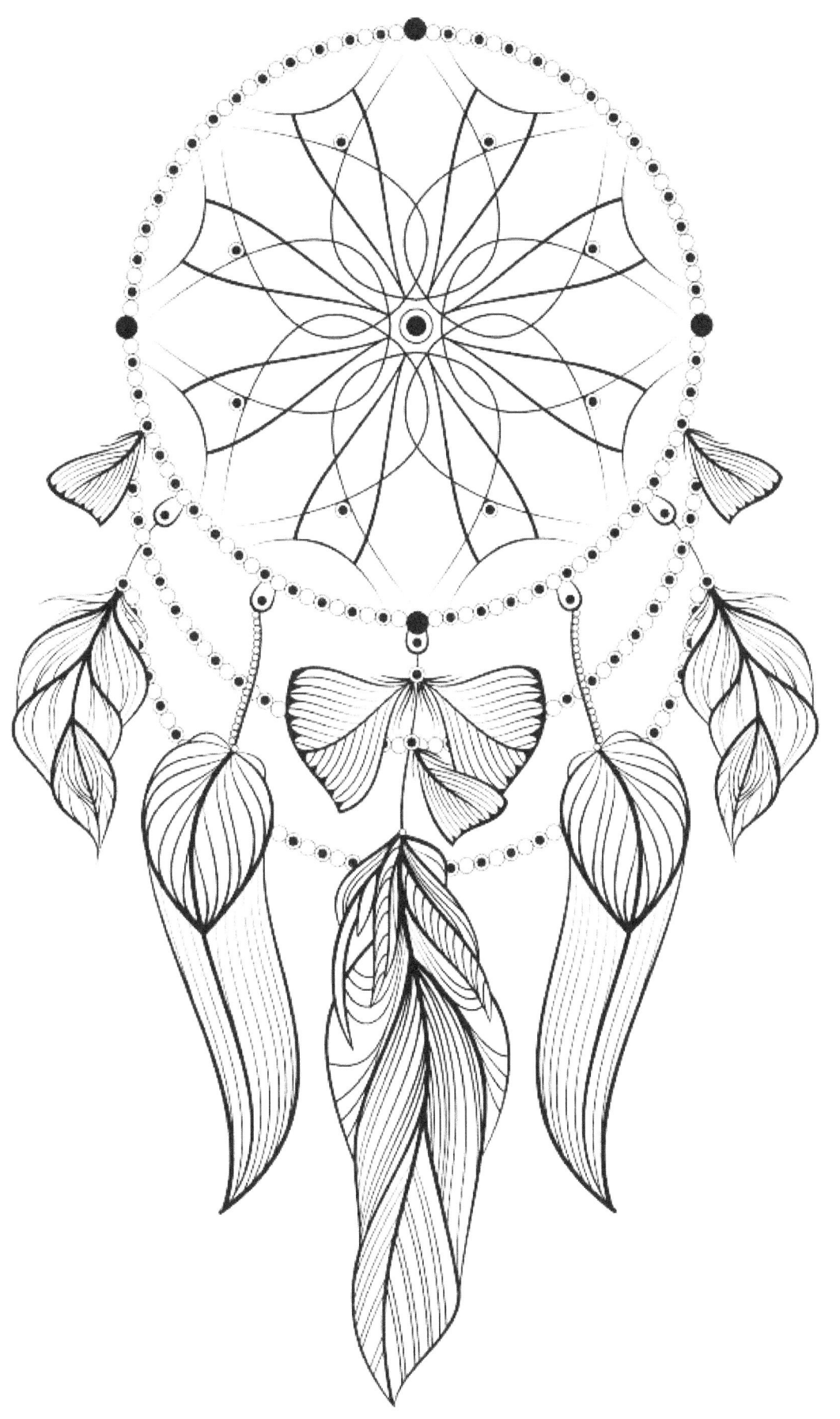

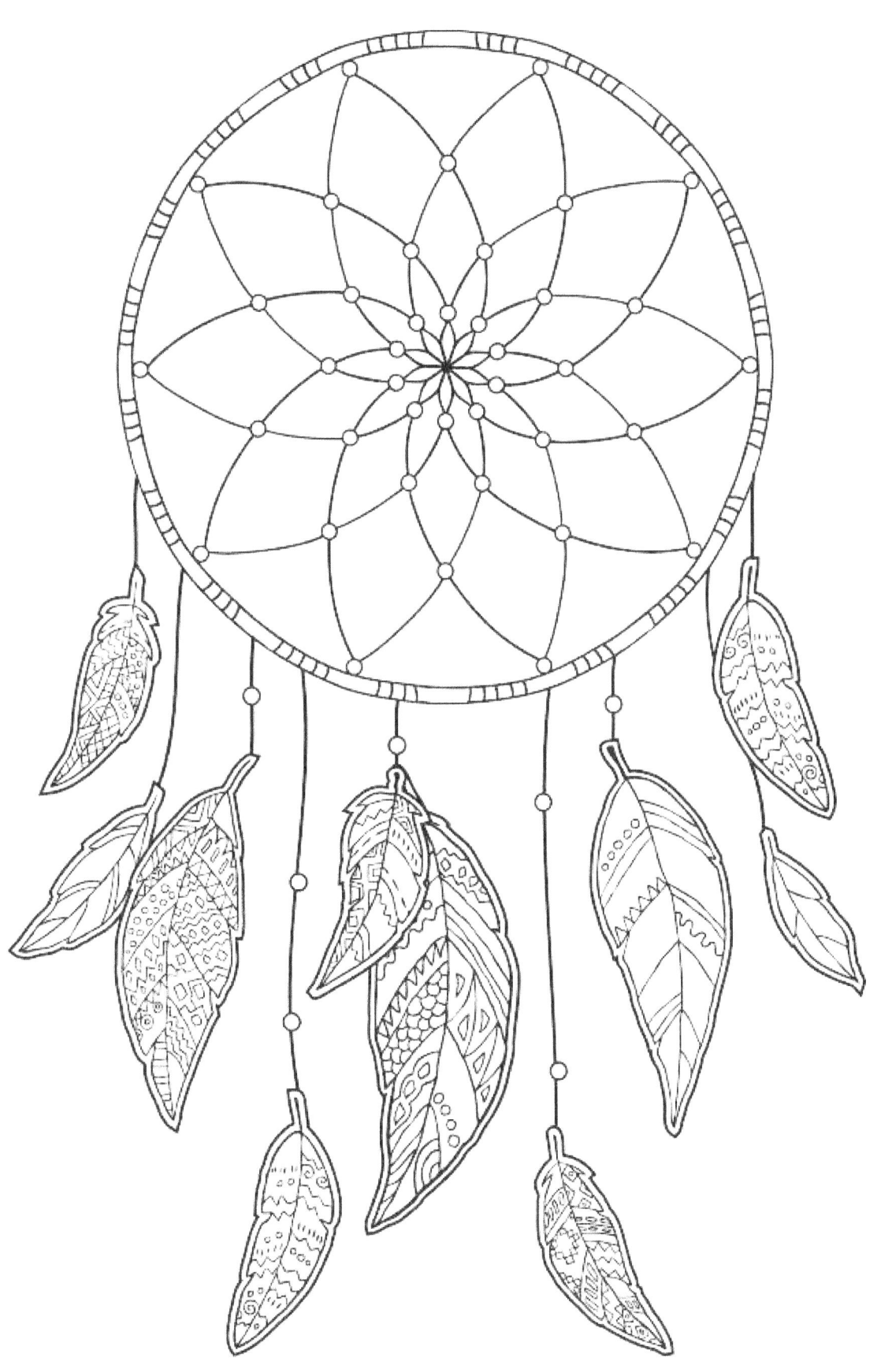

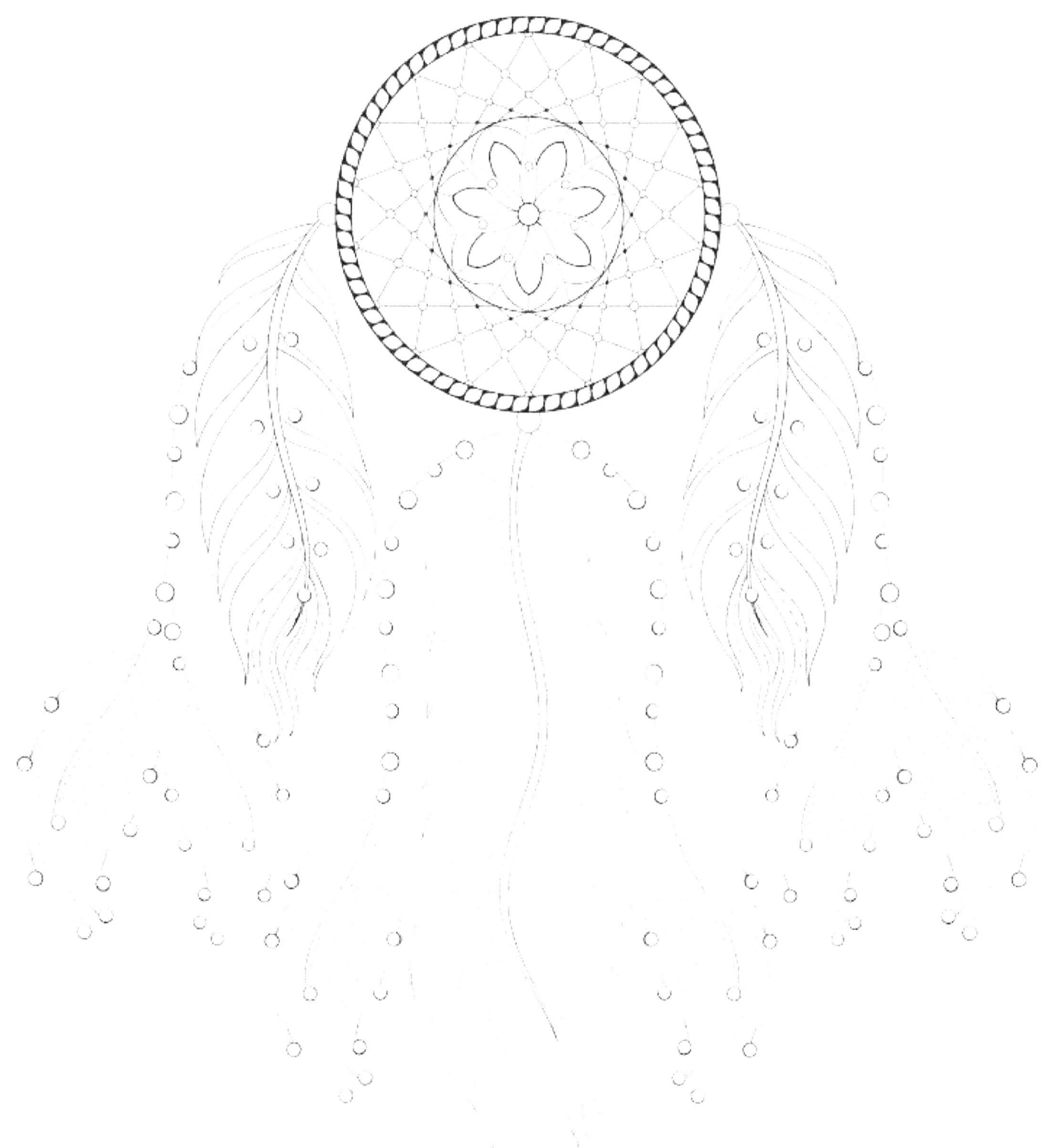

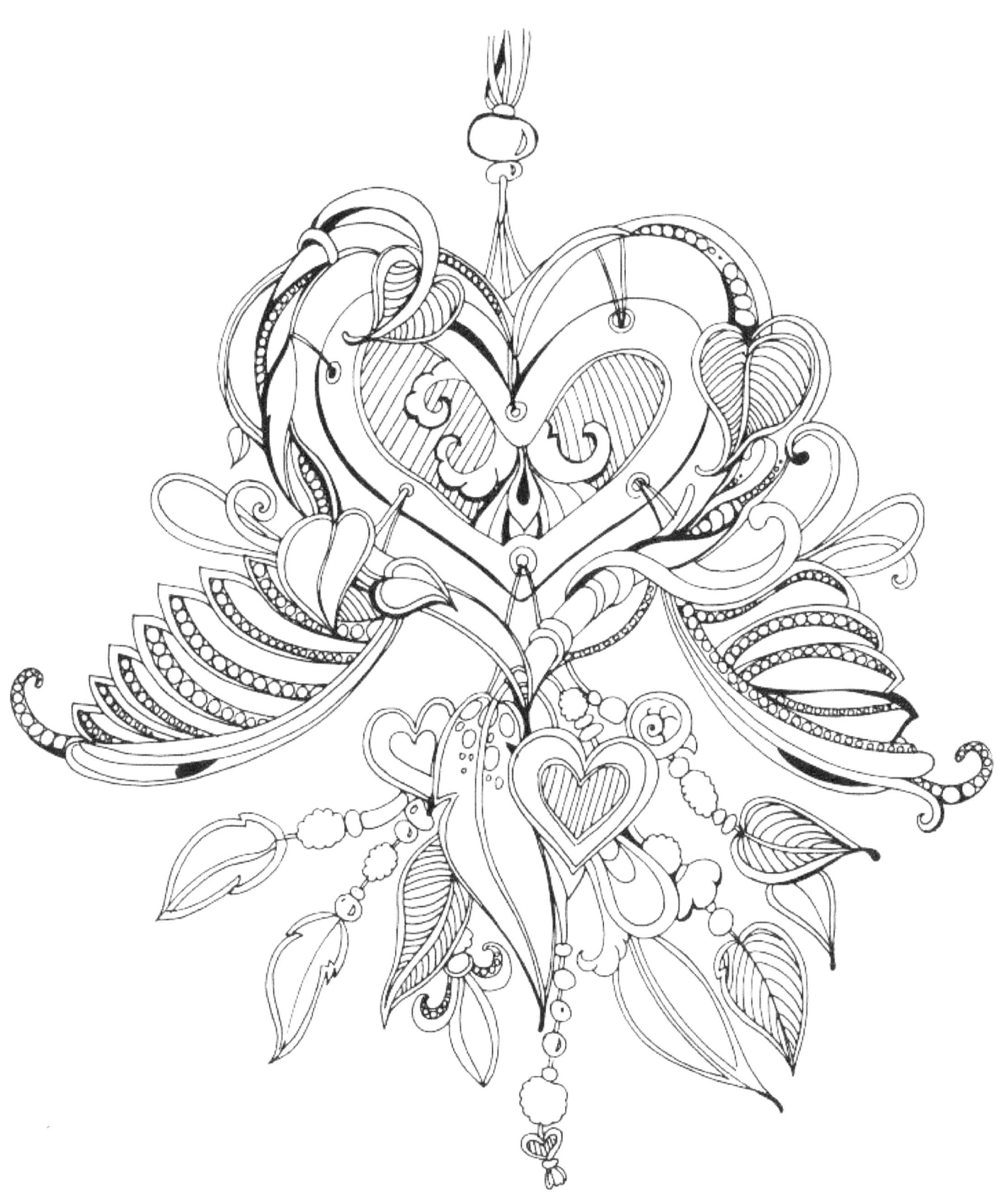

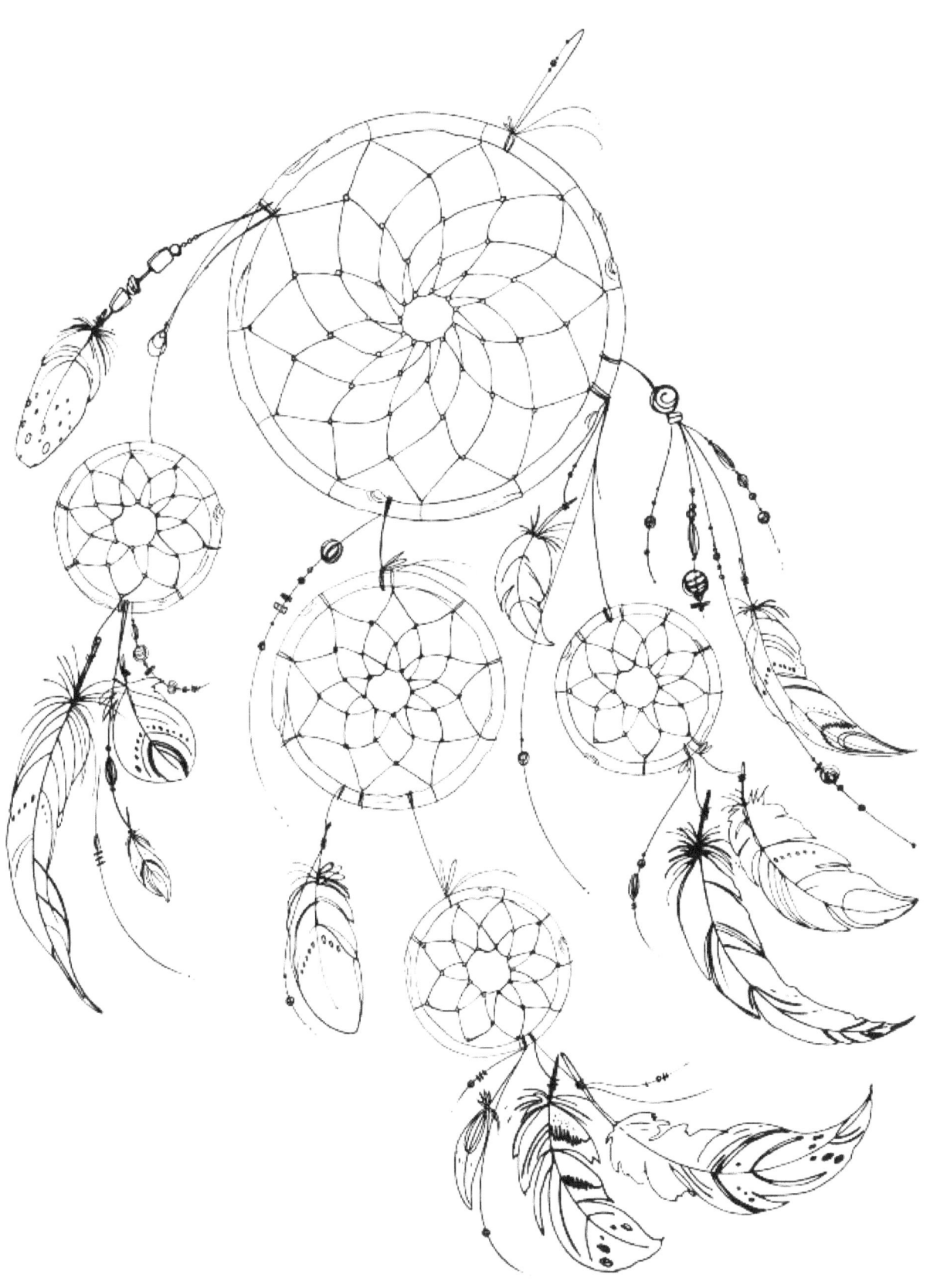

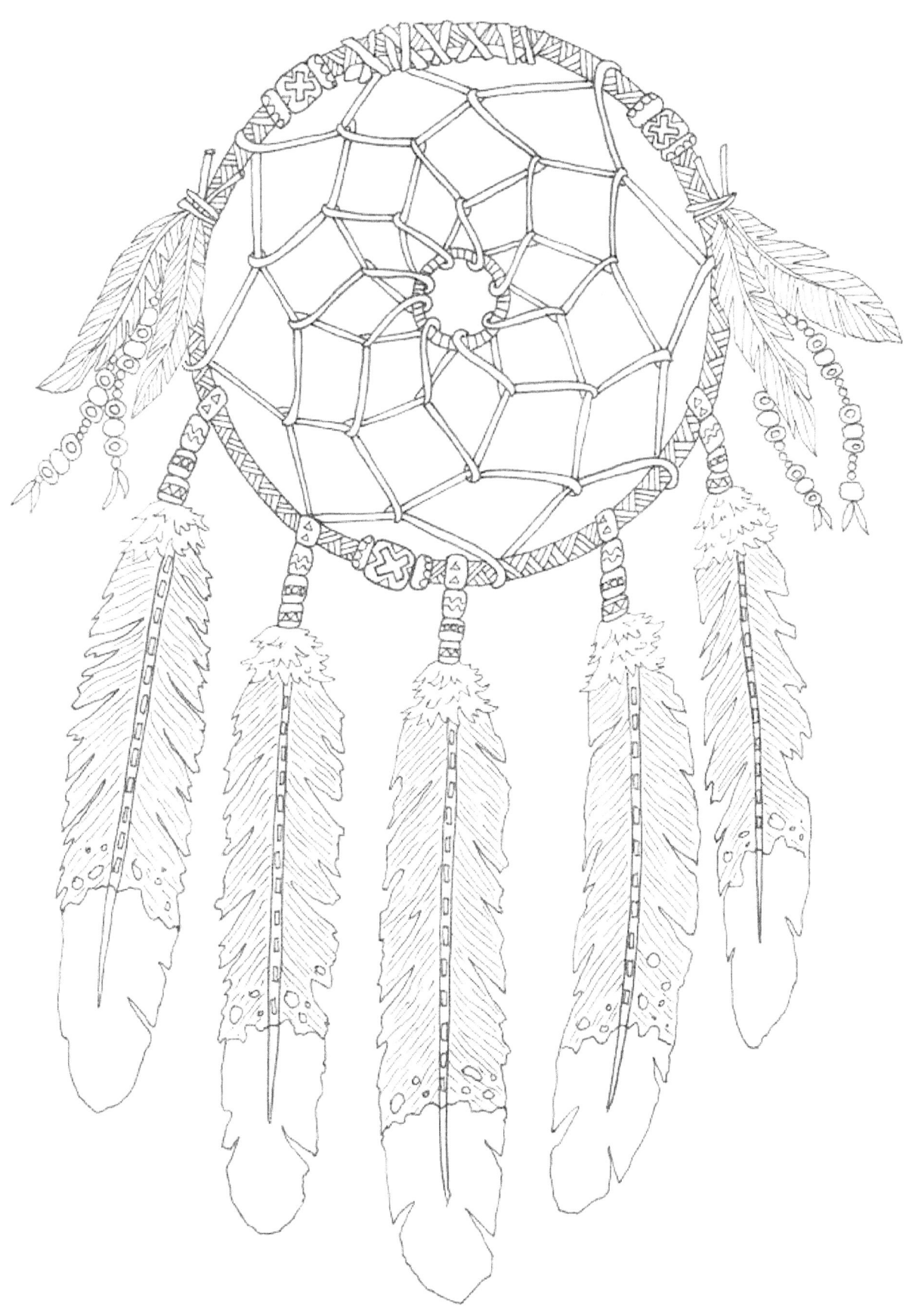

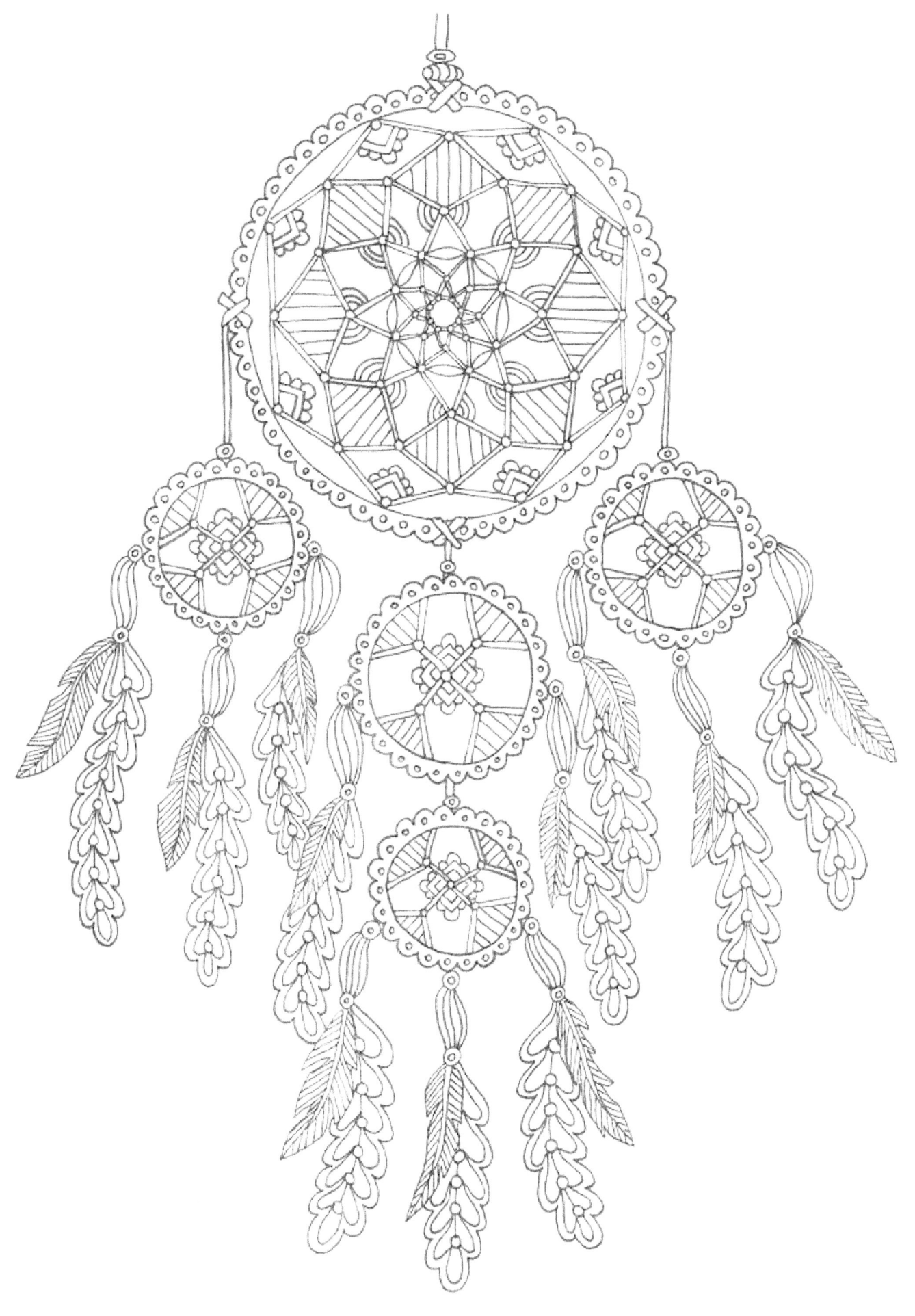

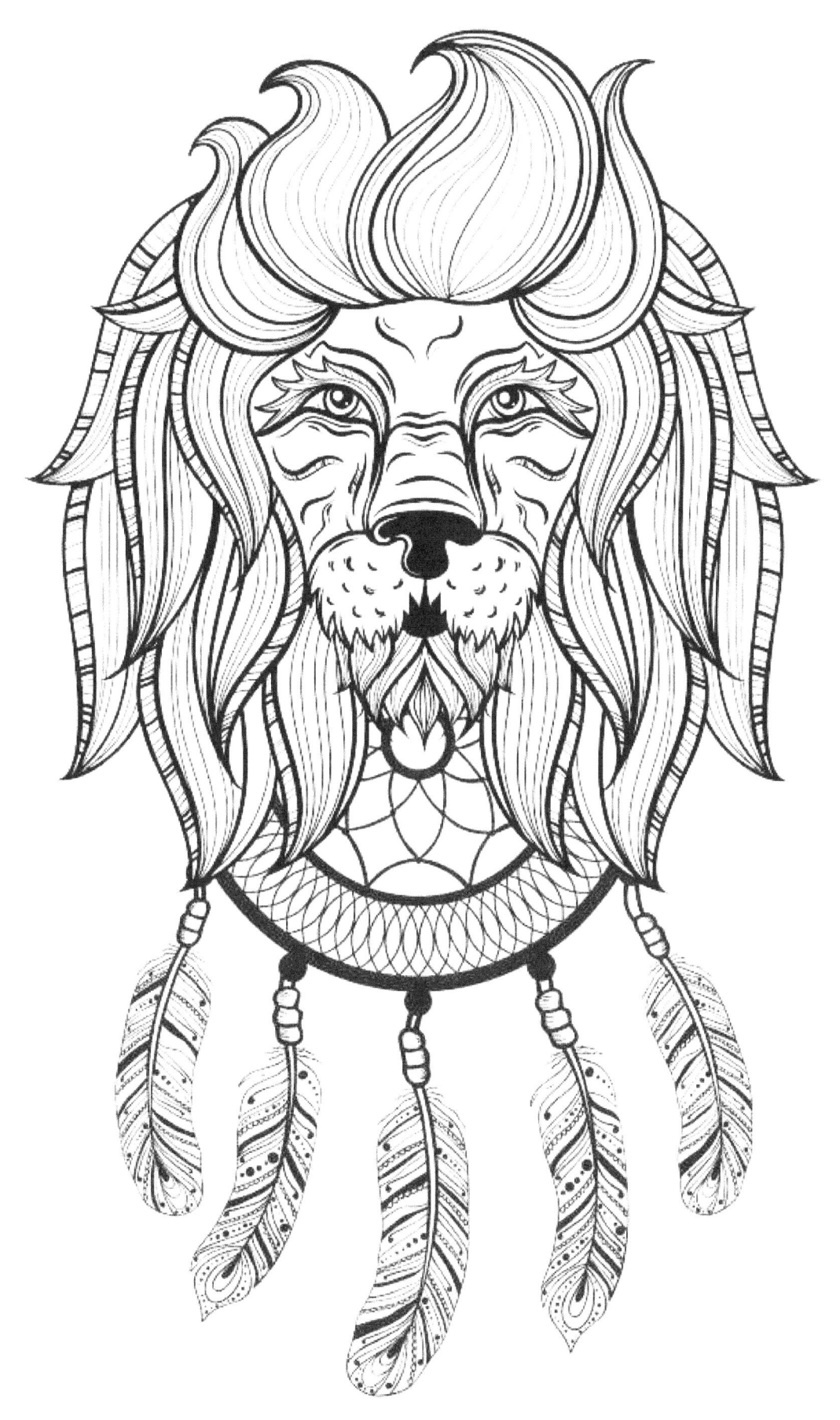

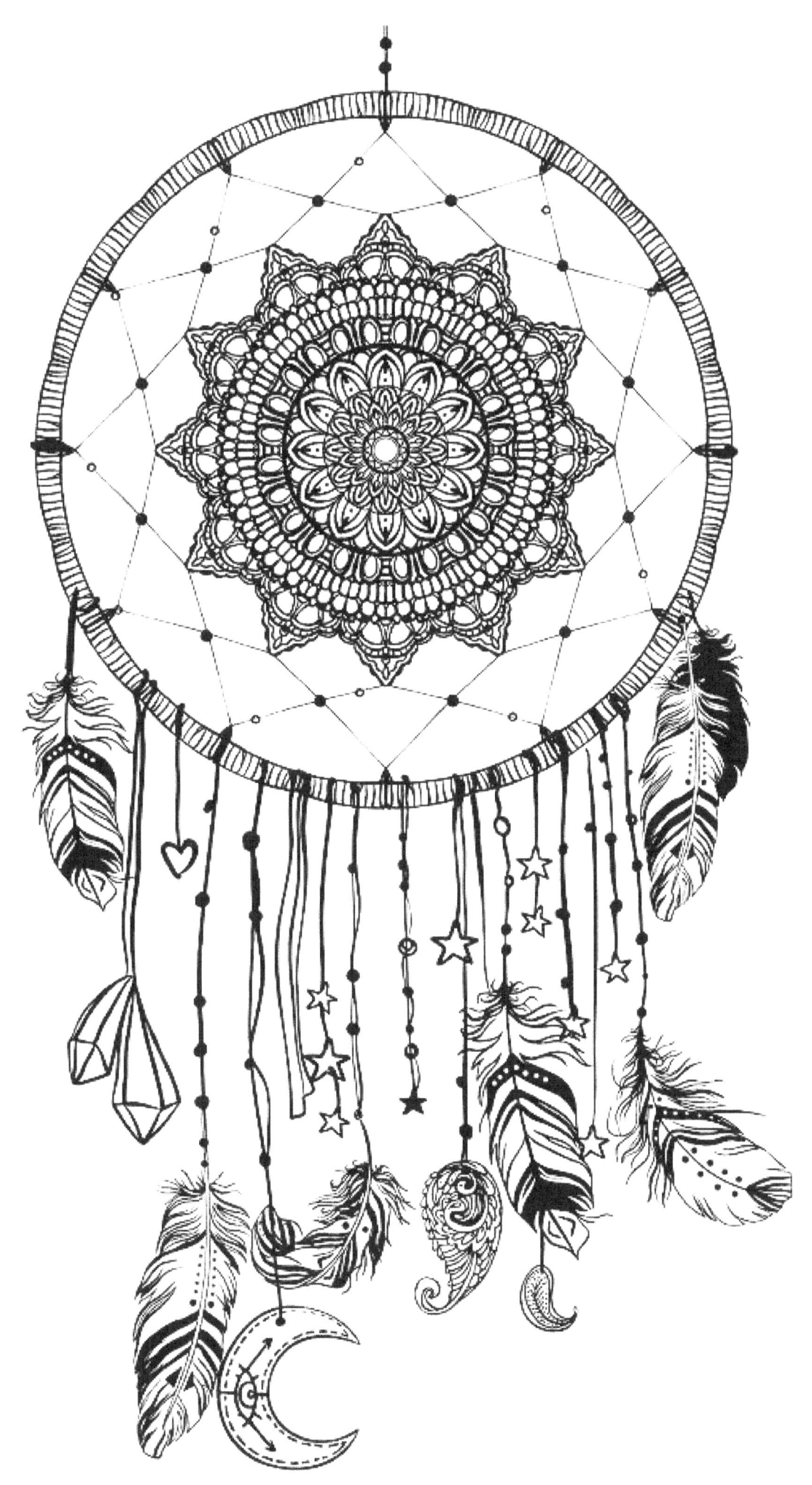

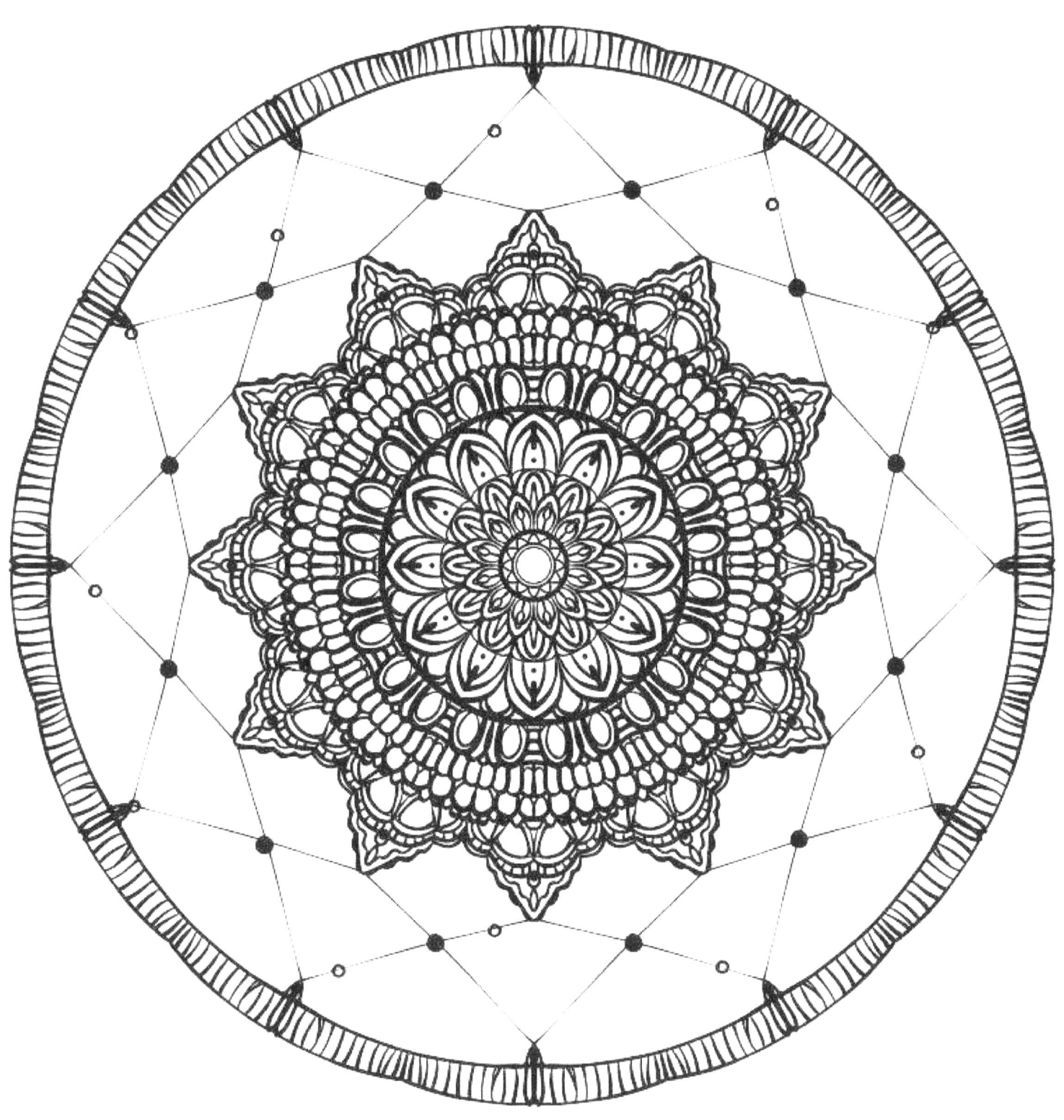

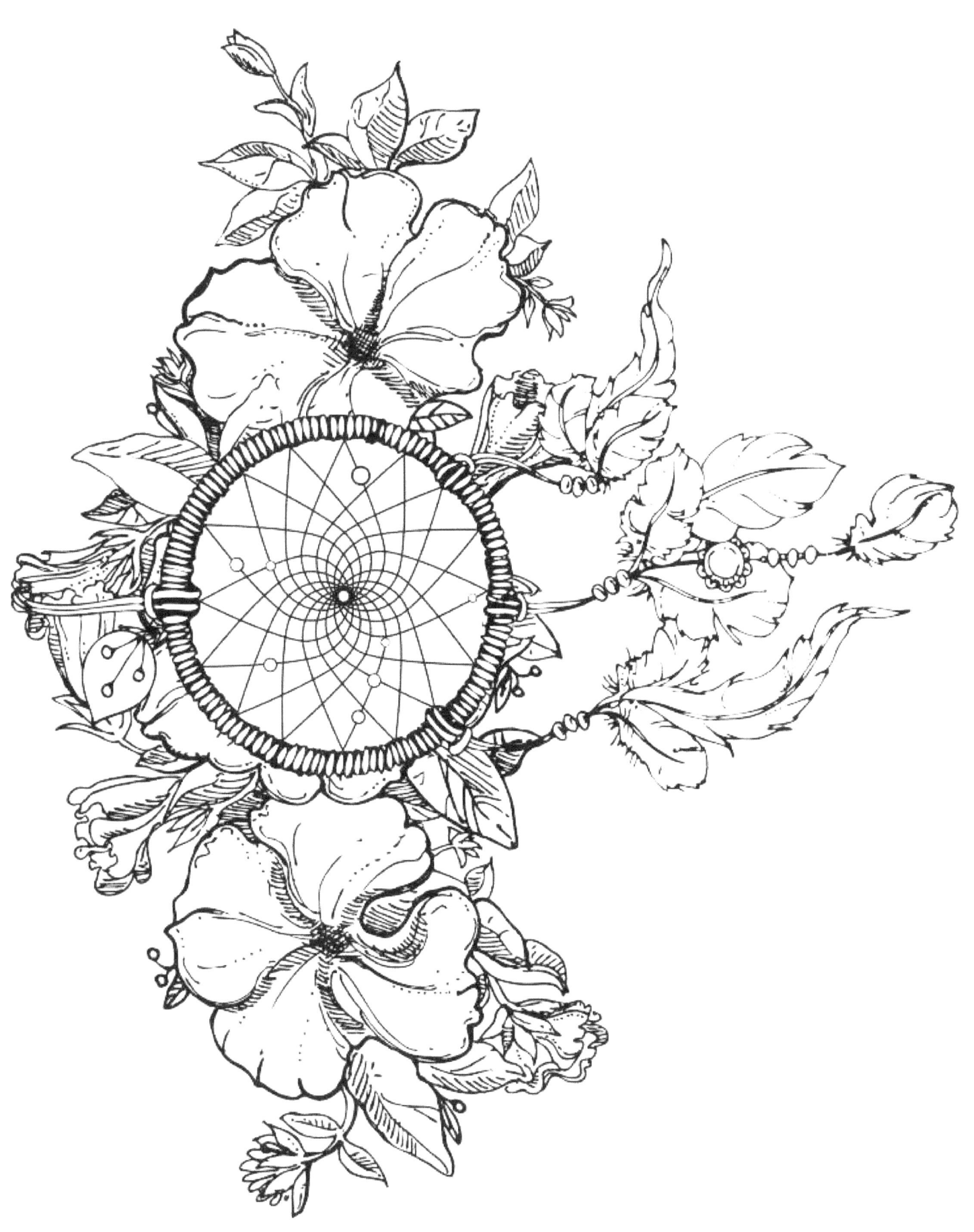

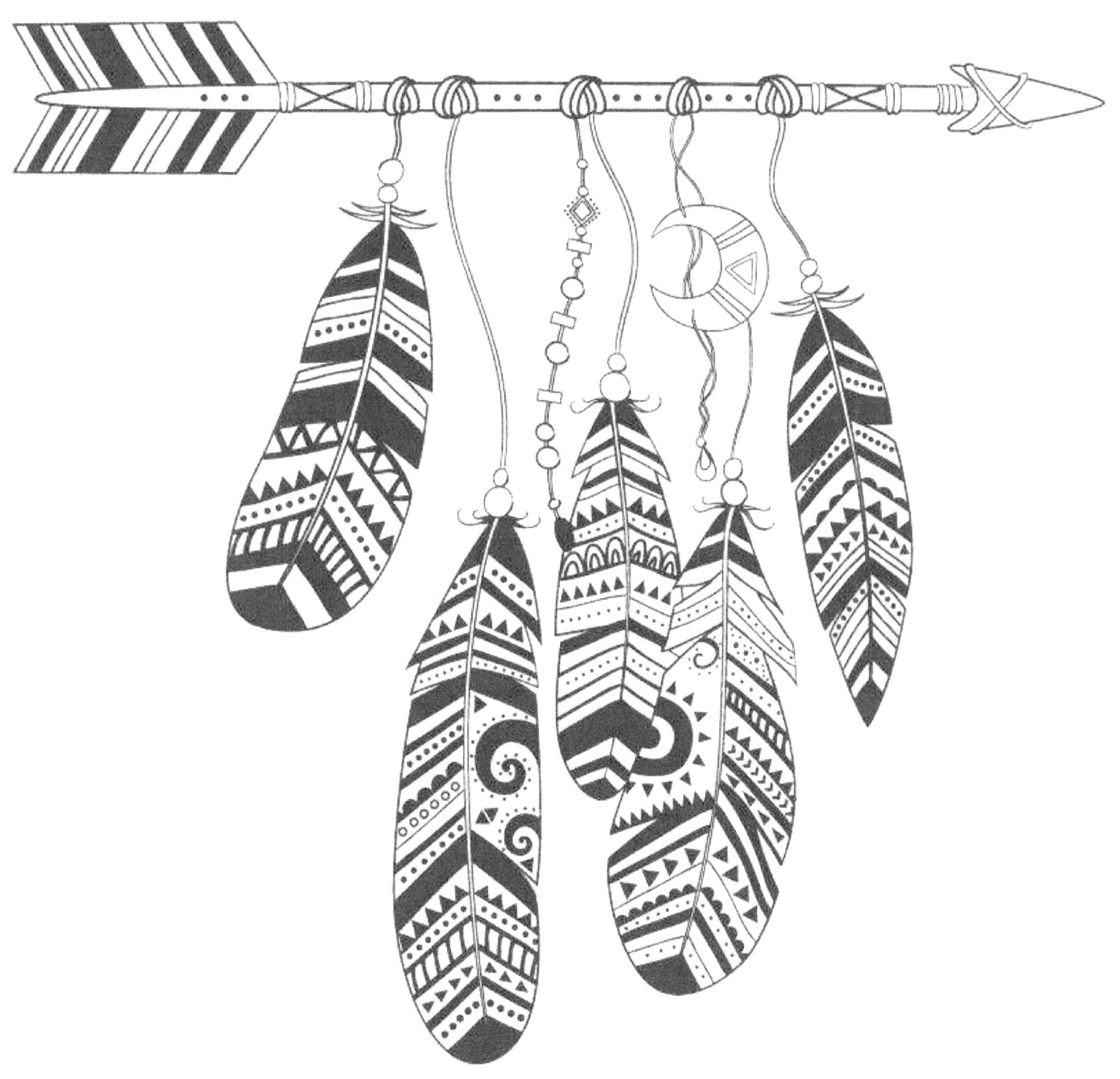

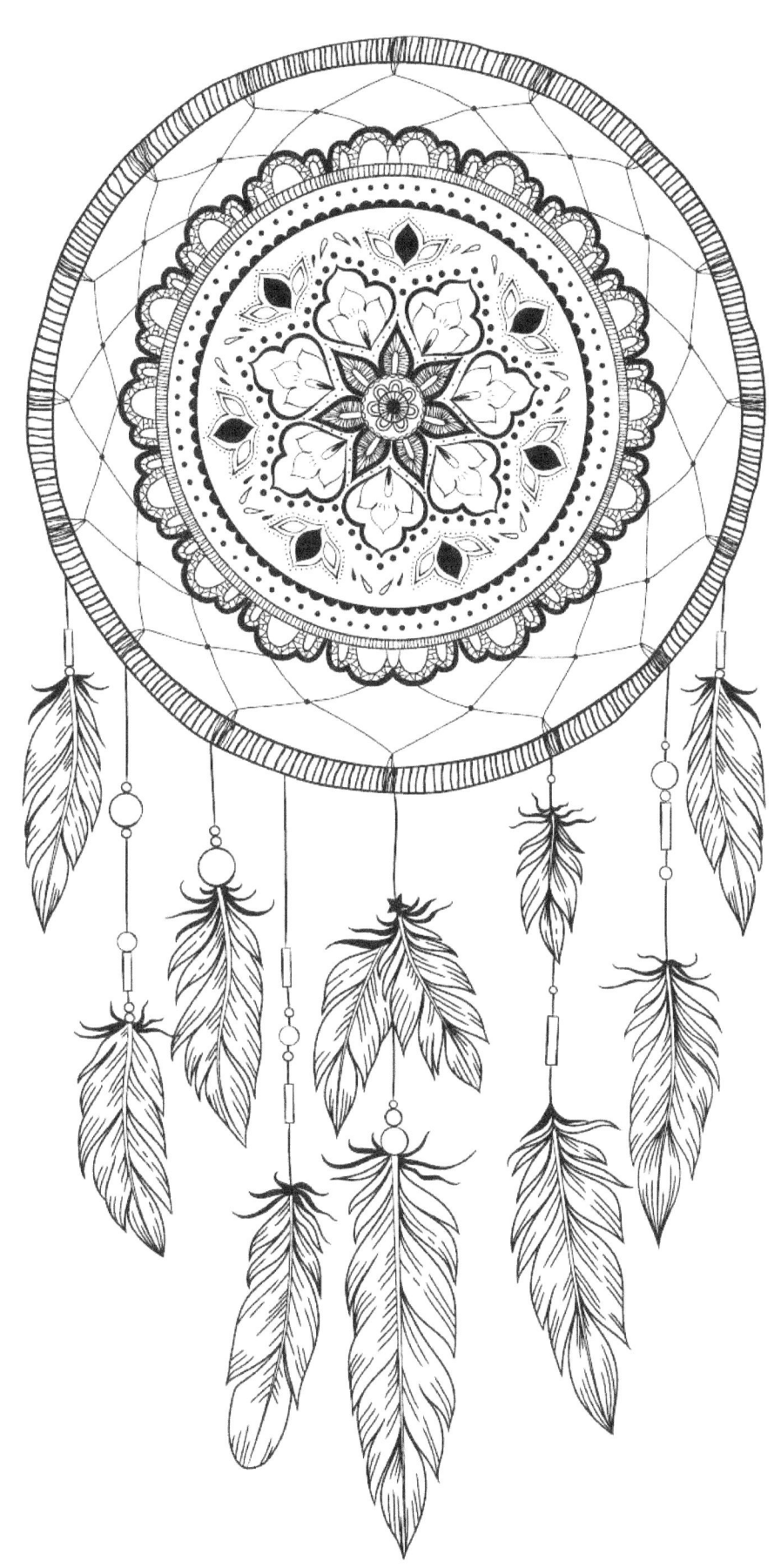

Free Surprise Bonus! We know how much native Americans loved their horses, so we thought it would be a nice surprise to add these beautiful horse coloring pages. Enjoy!

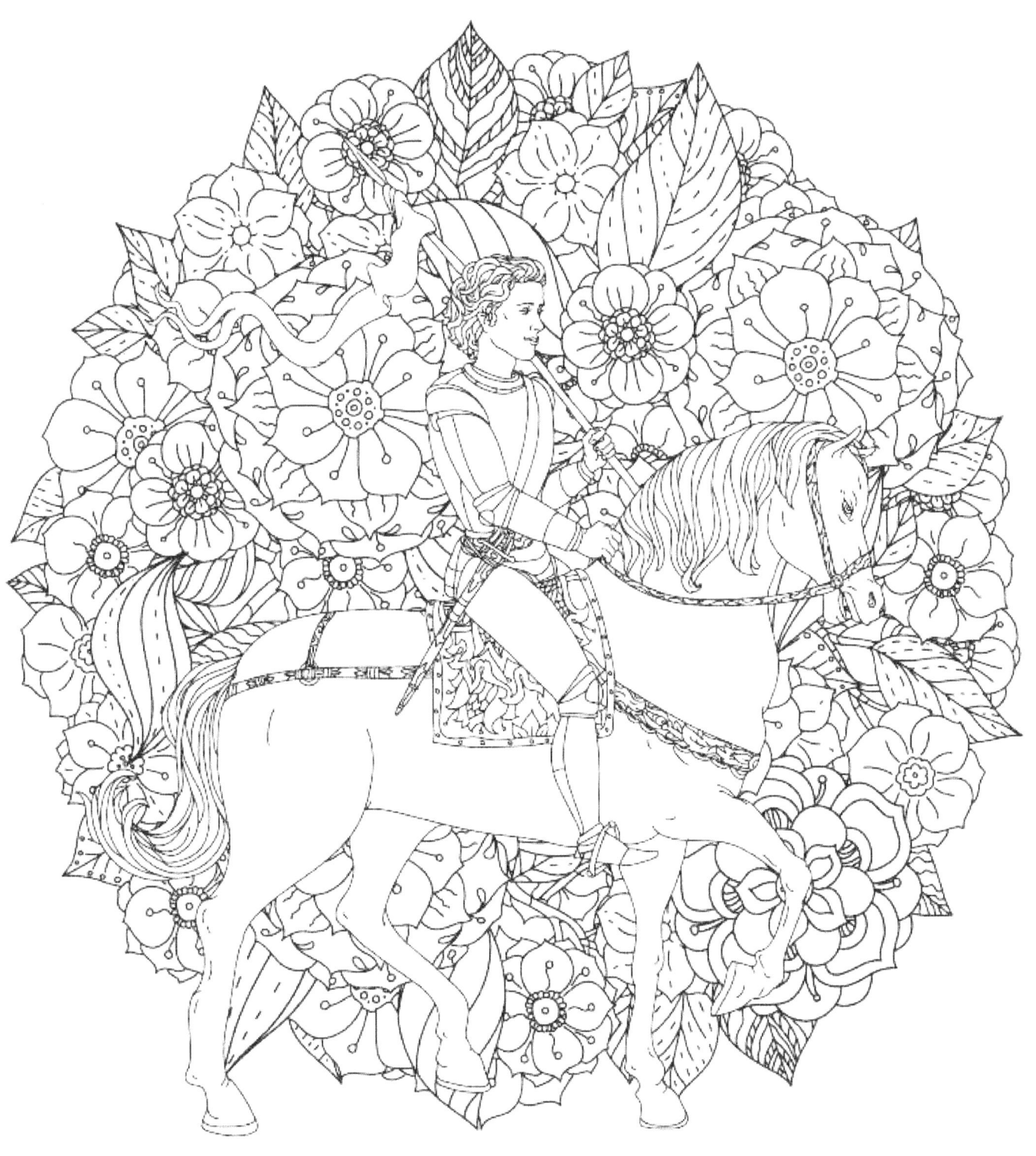

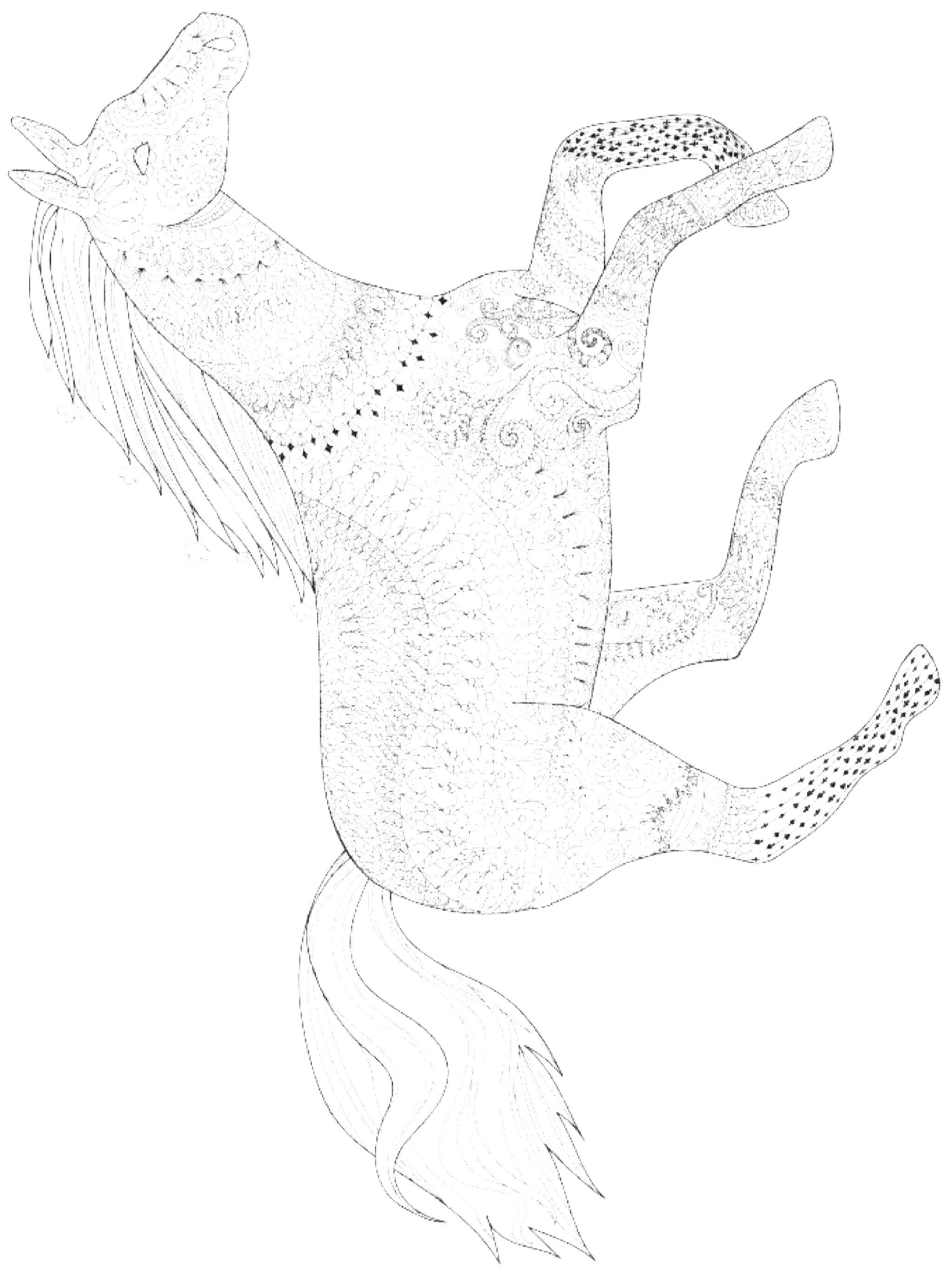

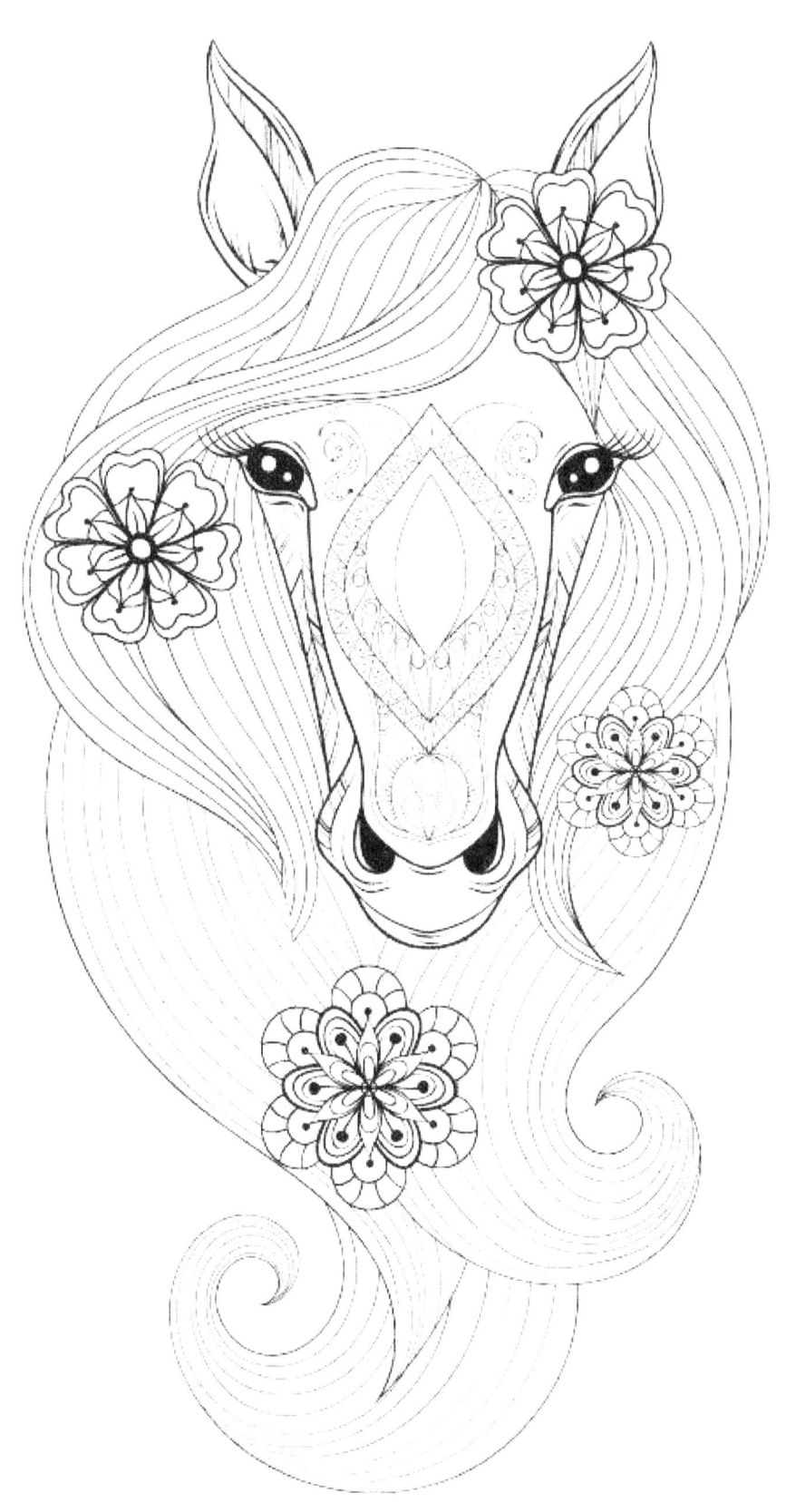

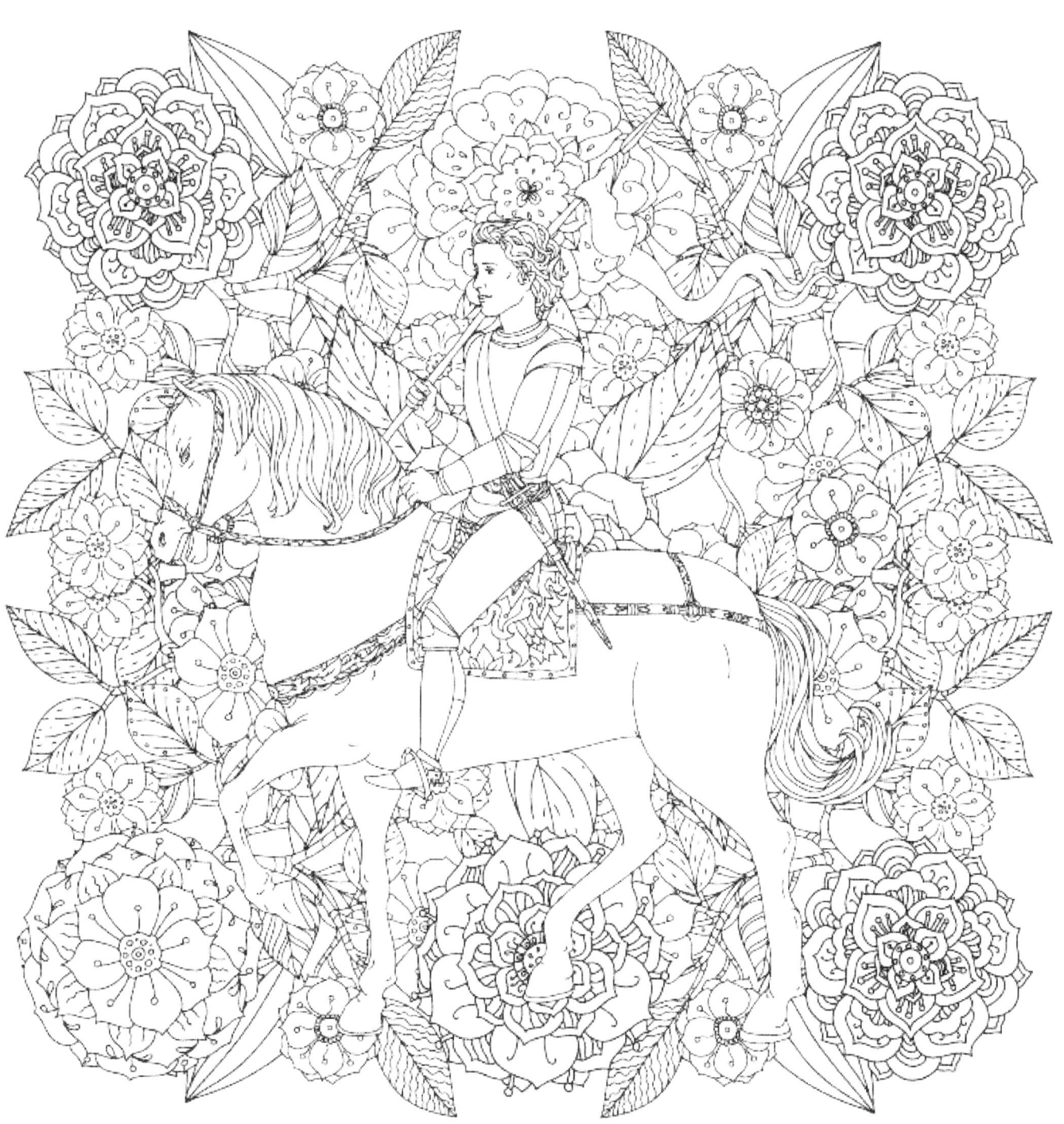

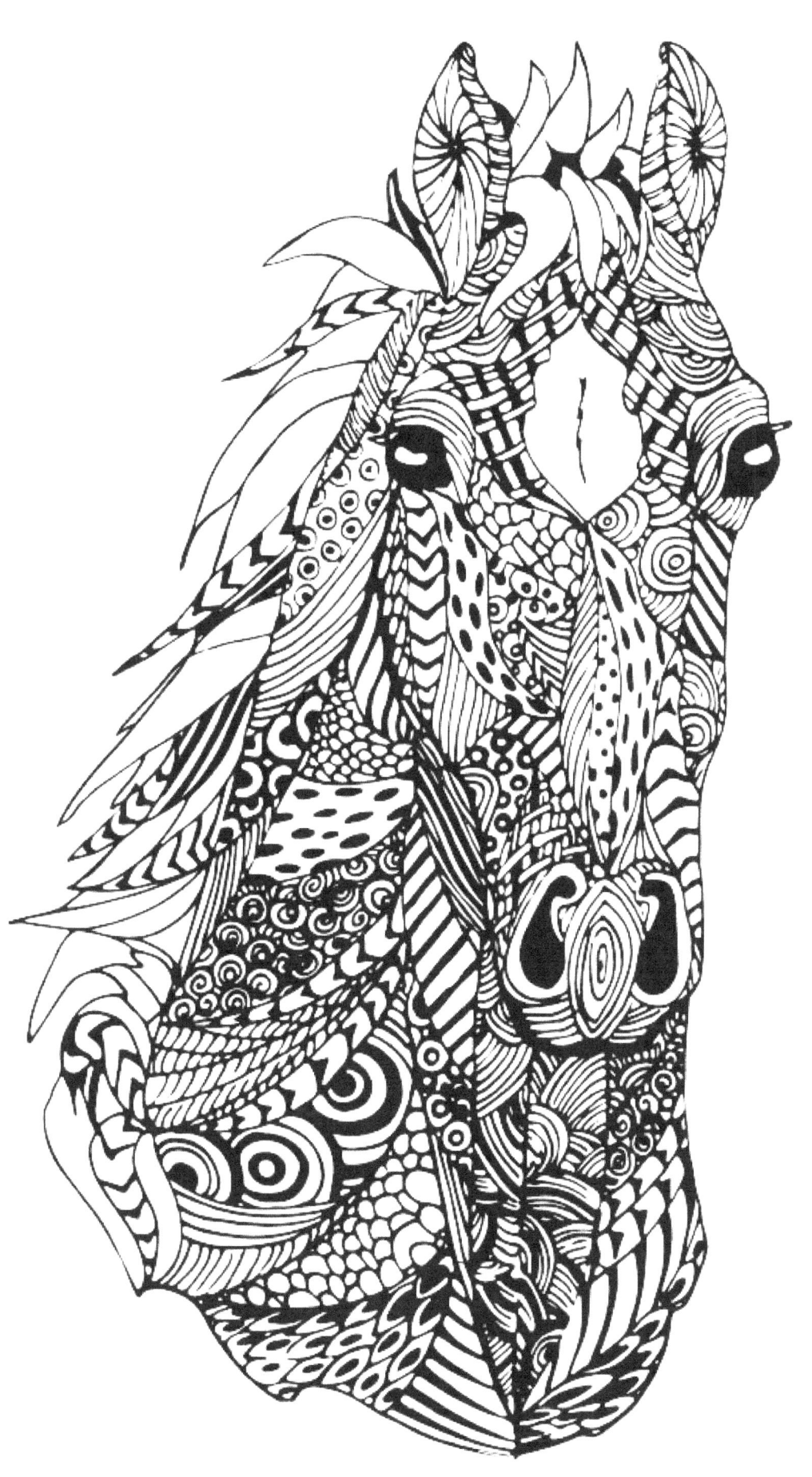

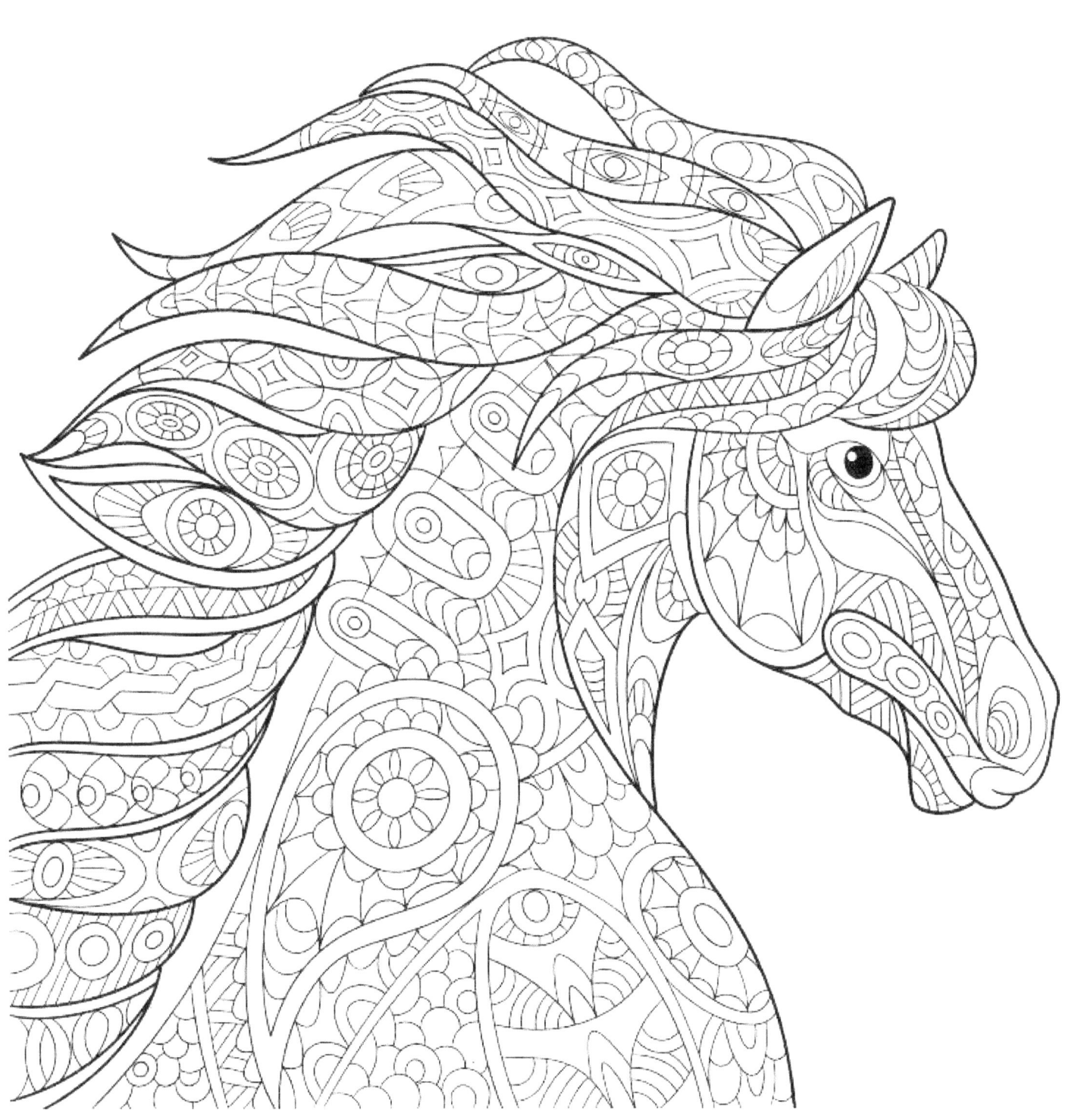

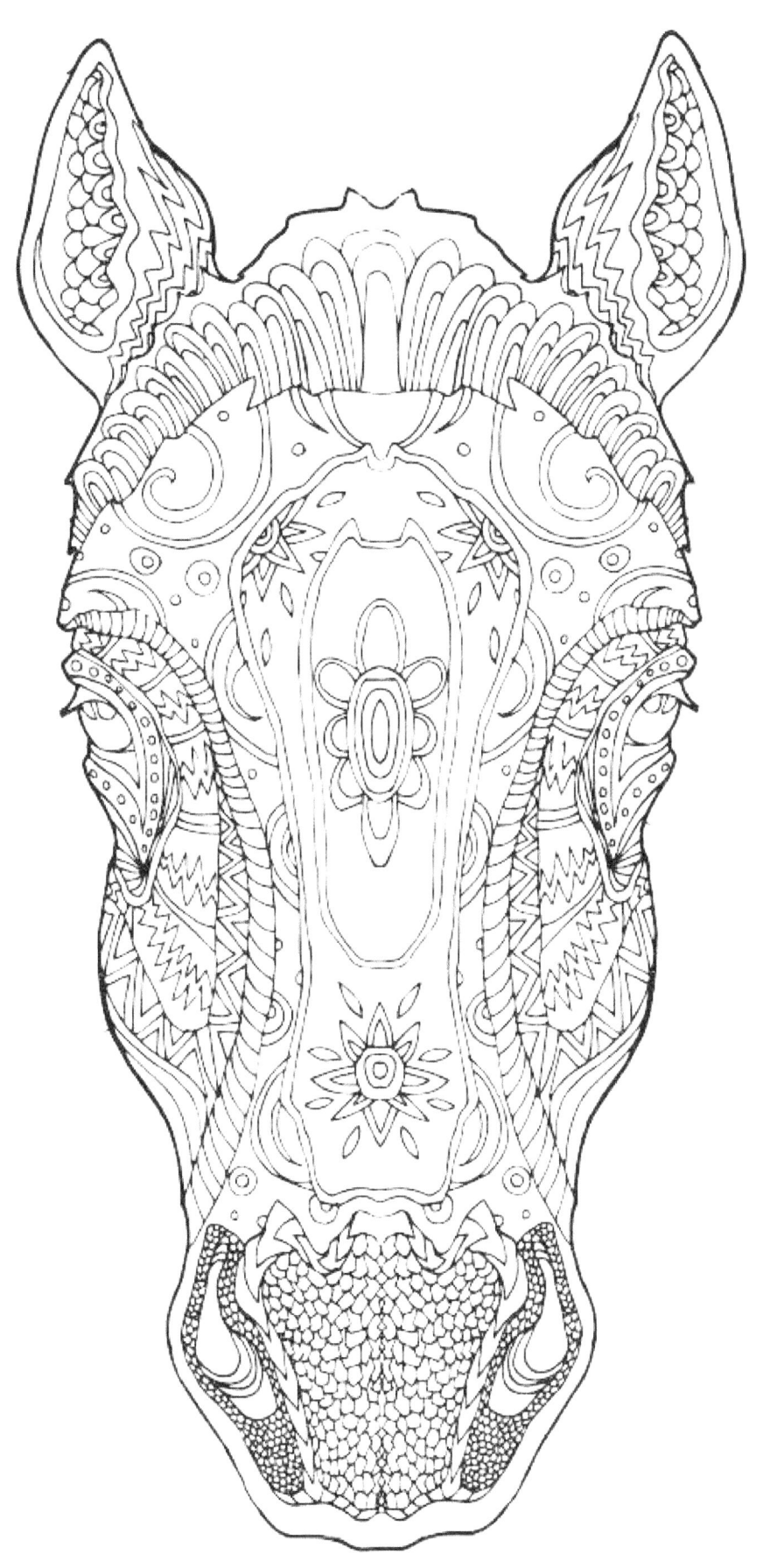

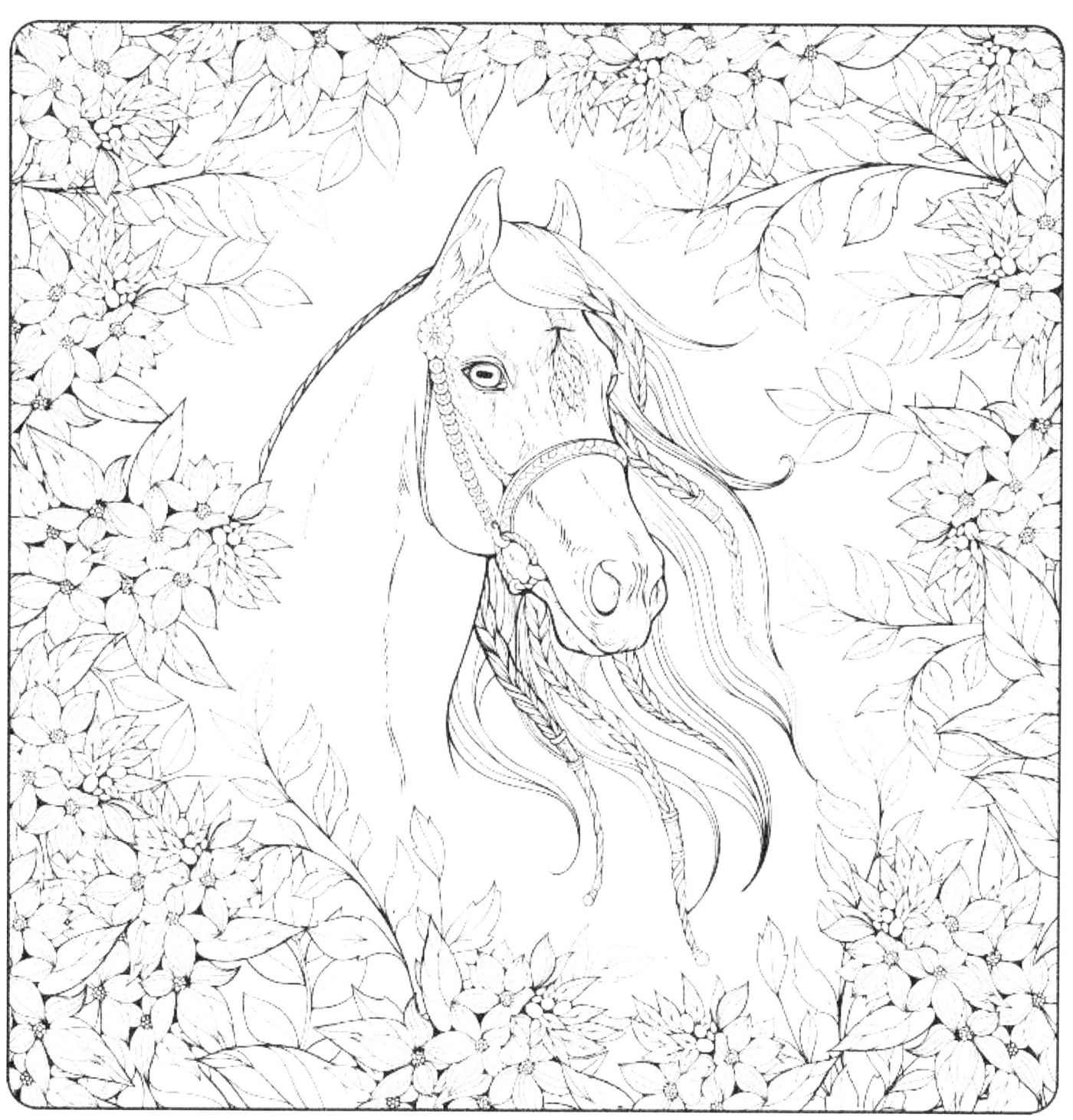

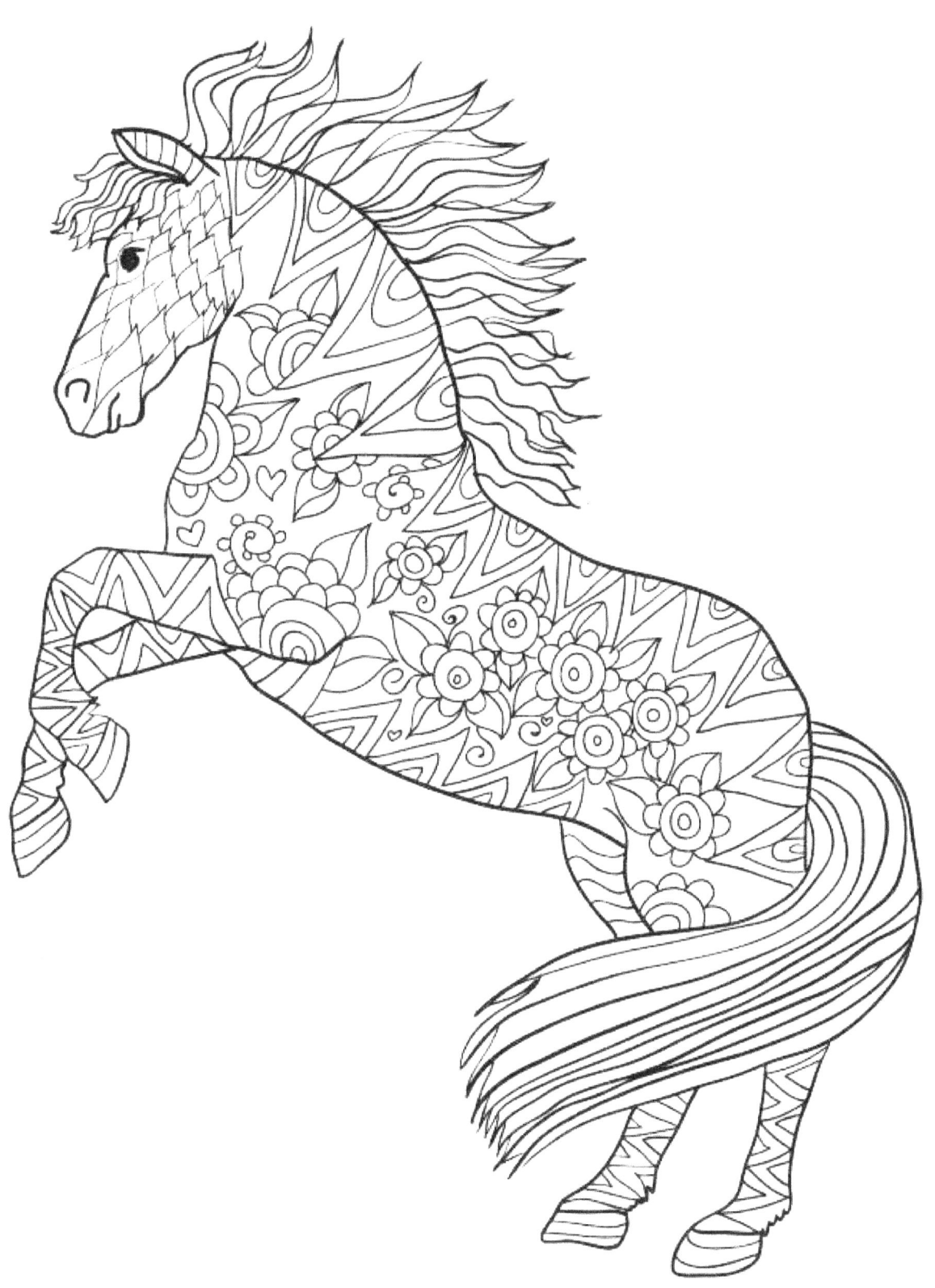

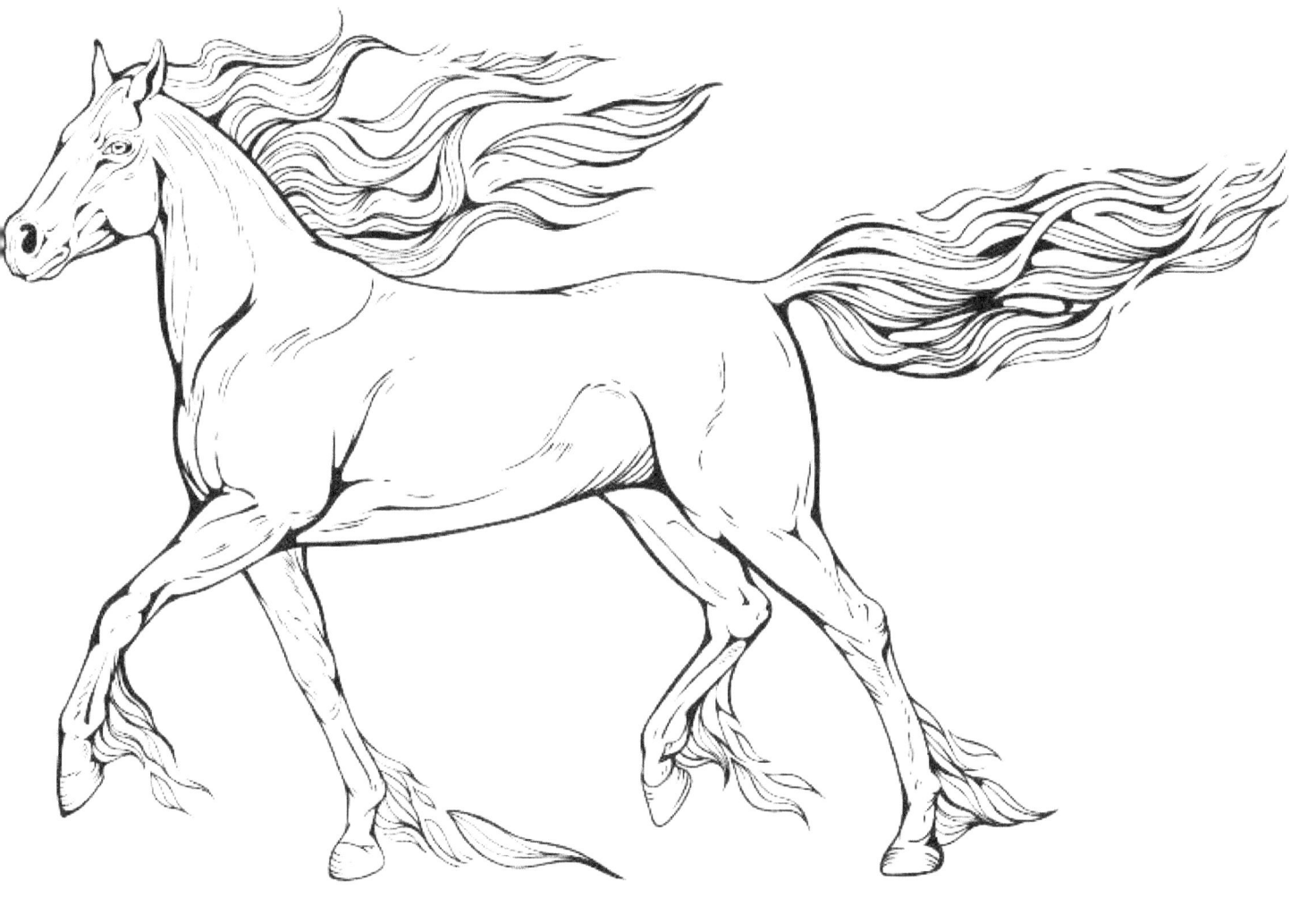

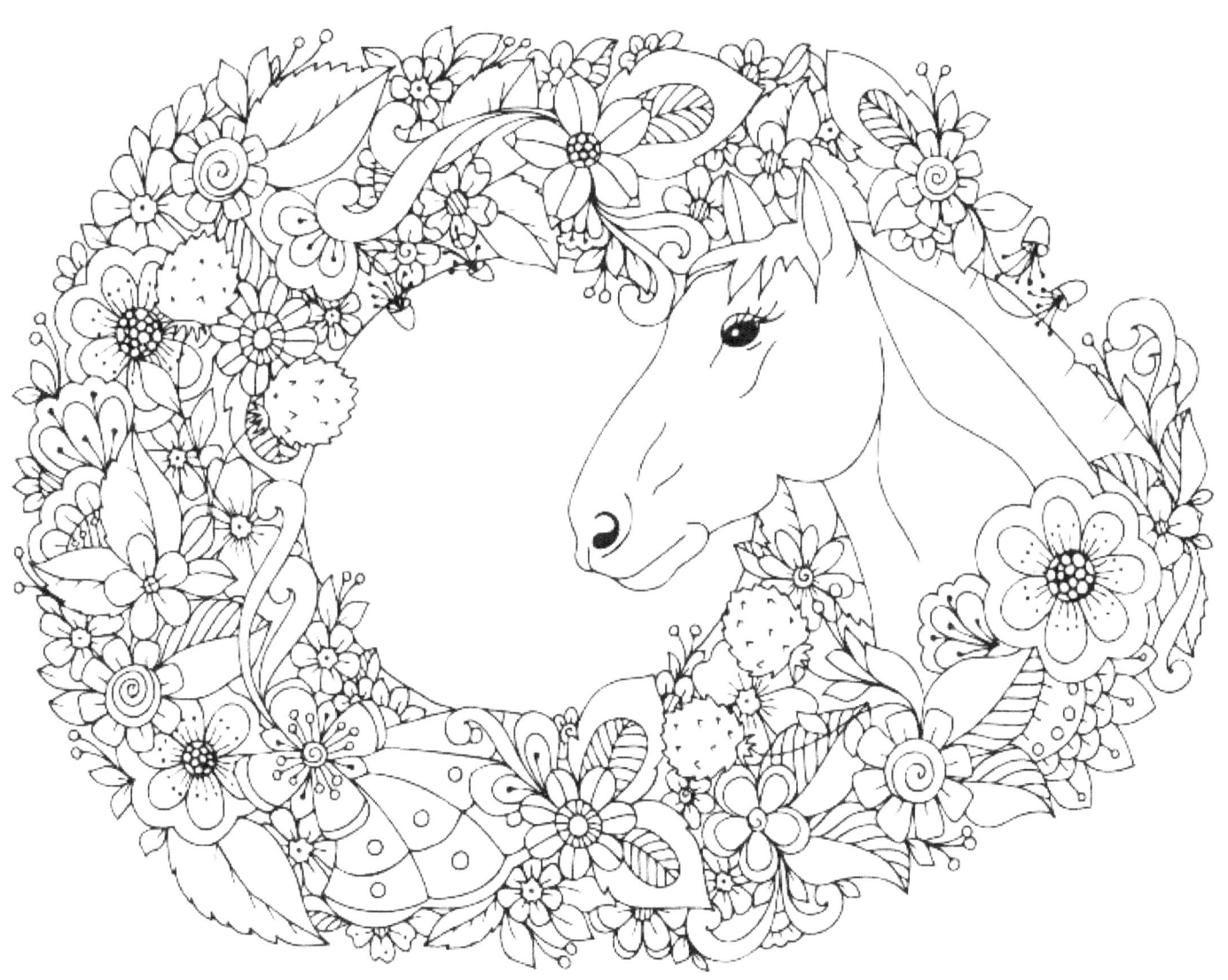

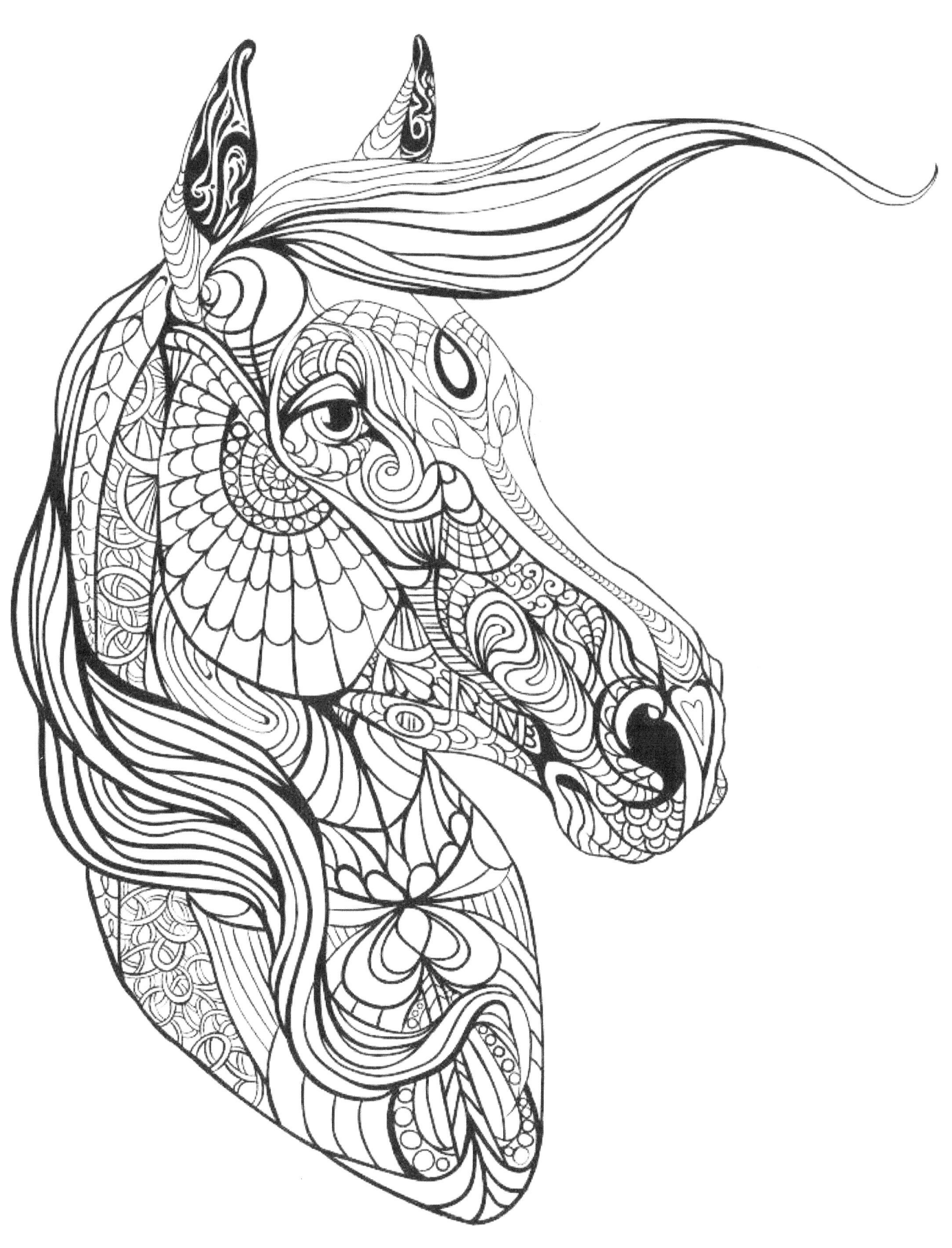

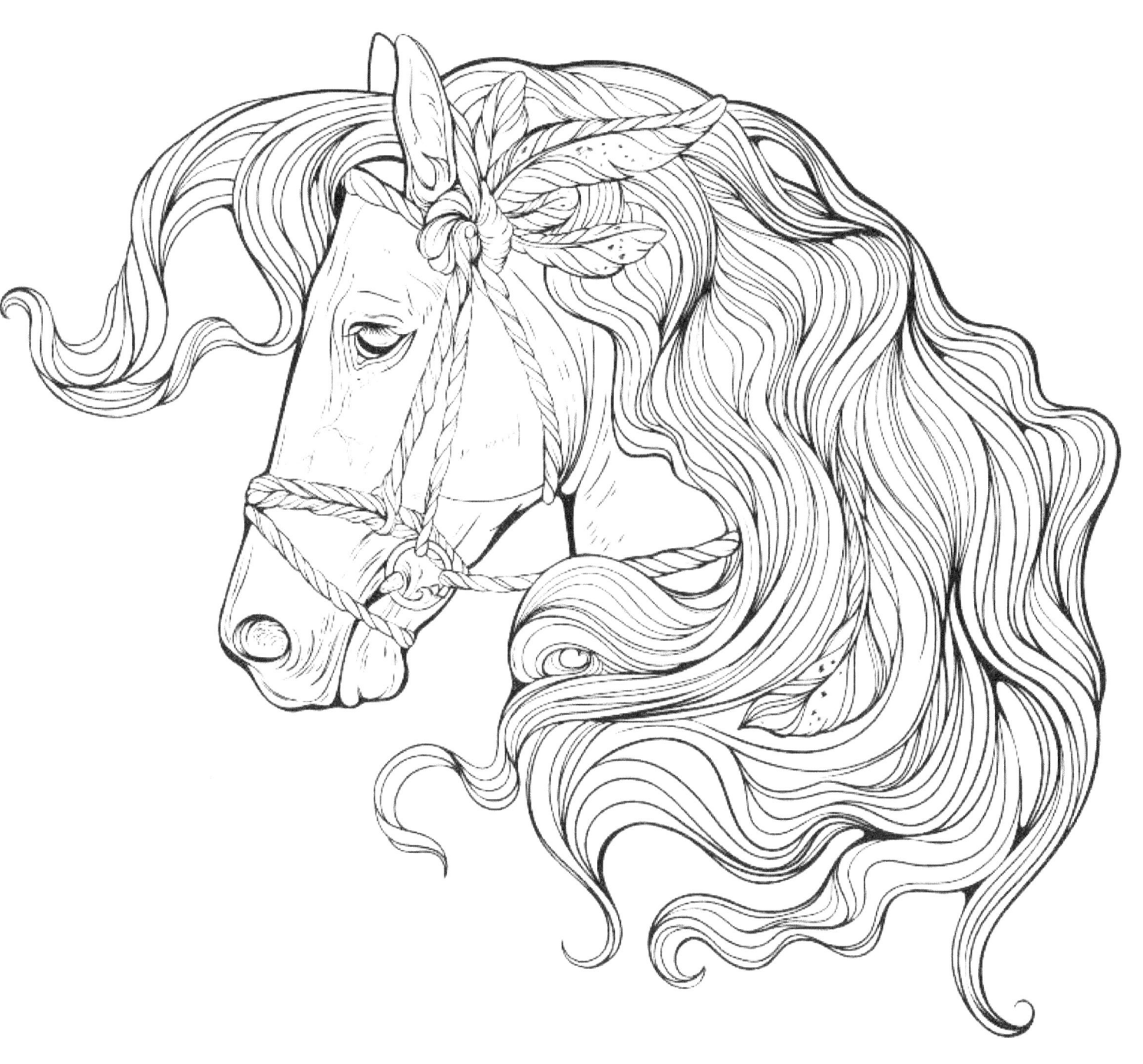

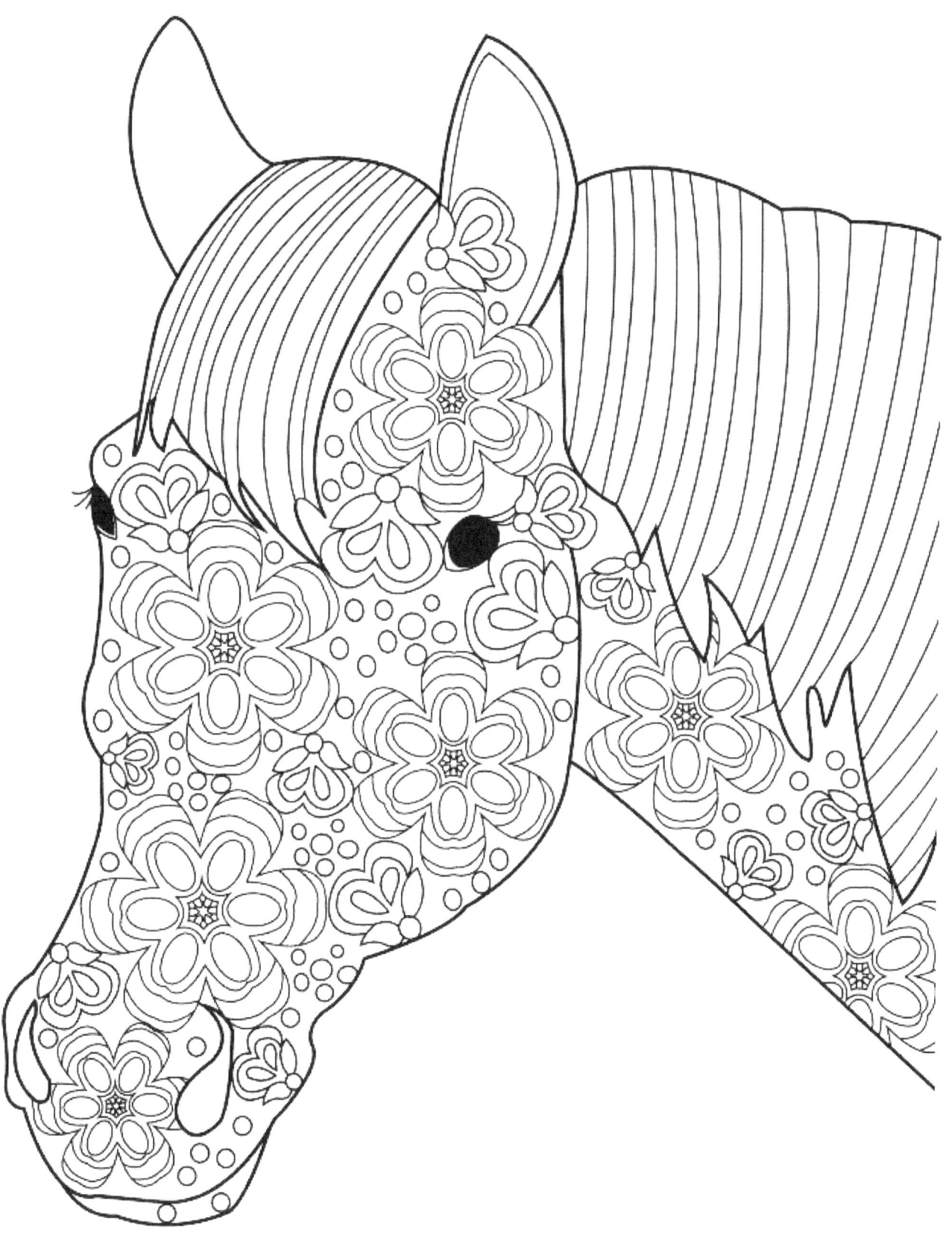

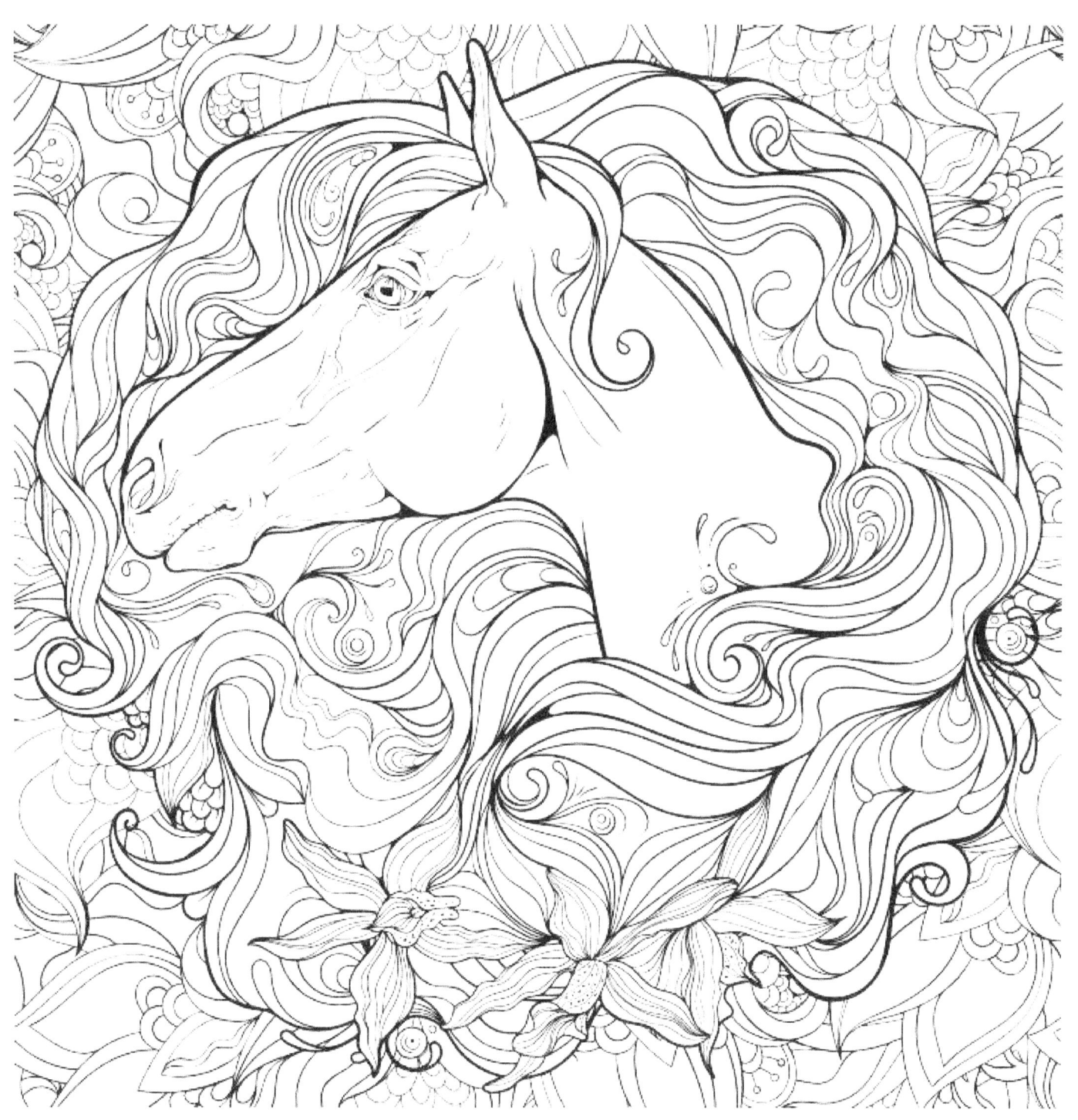

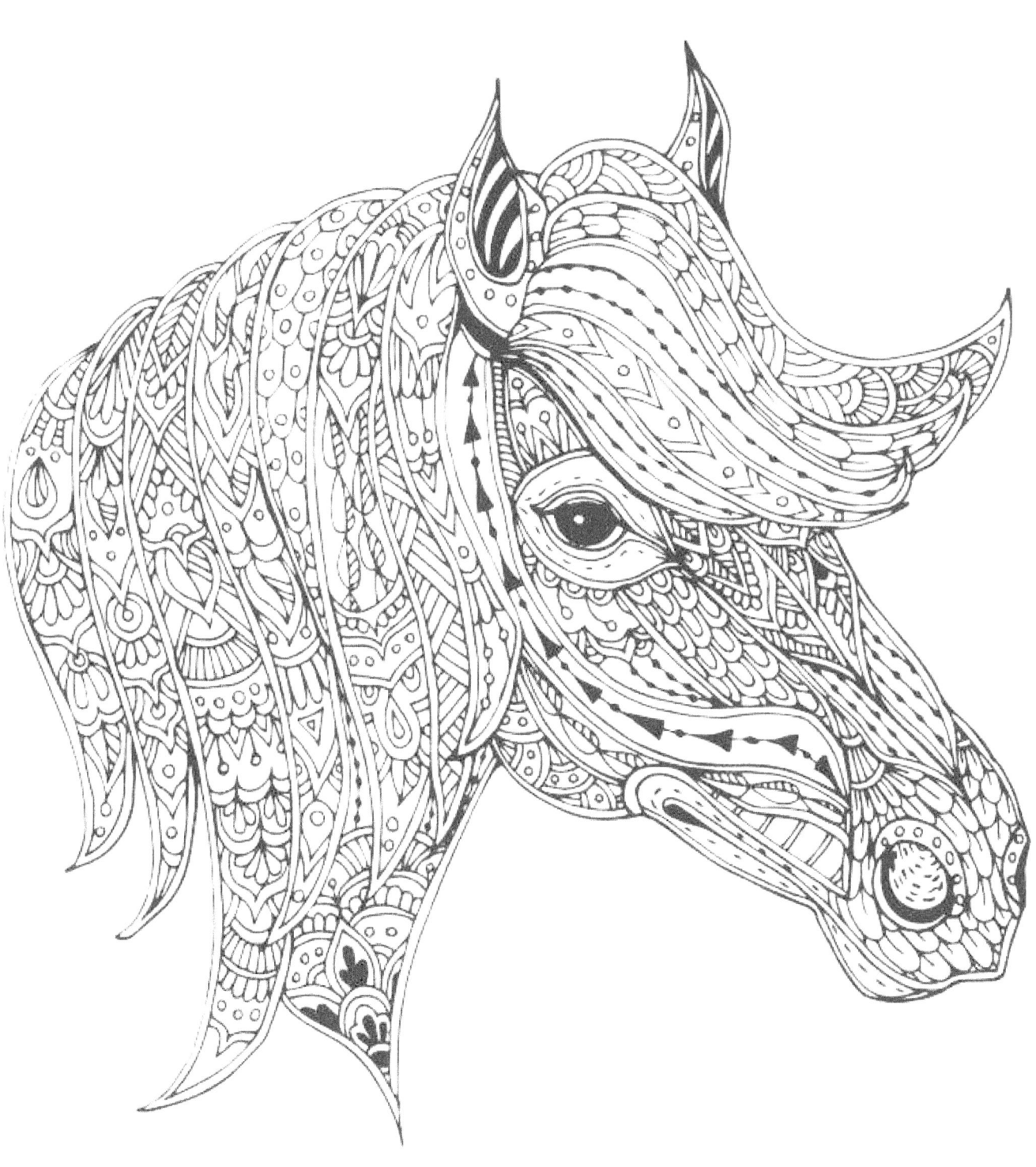

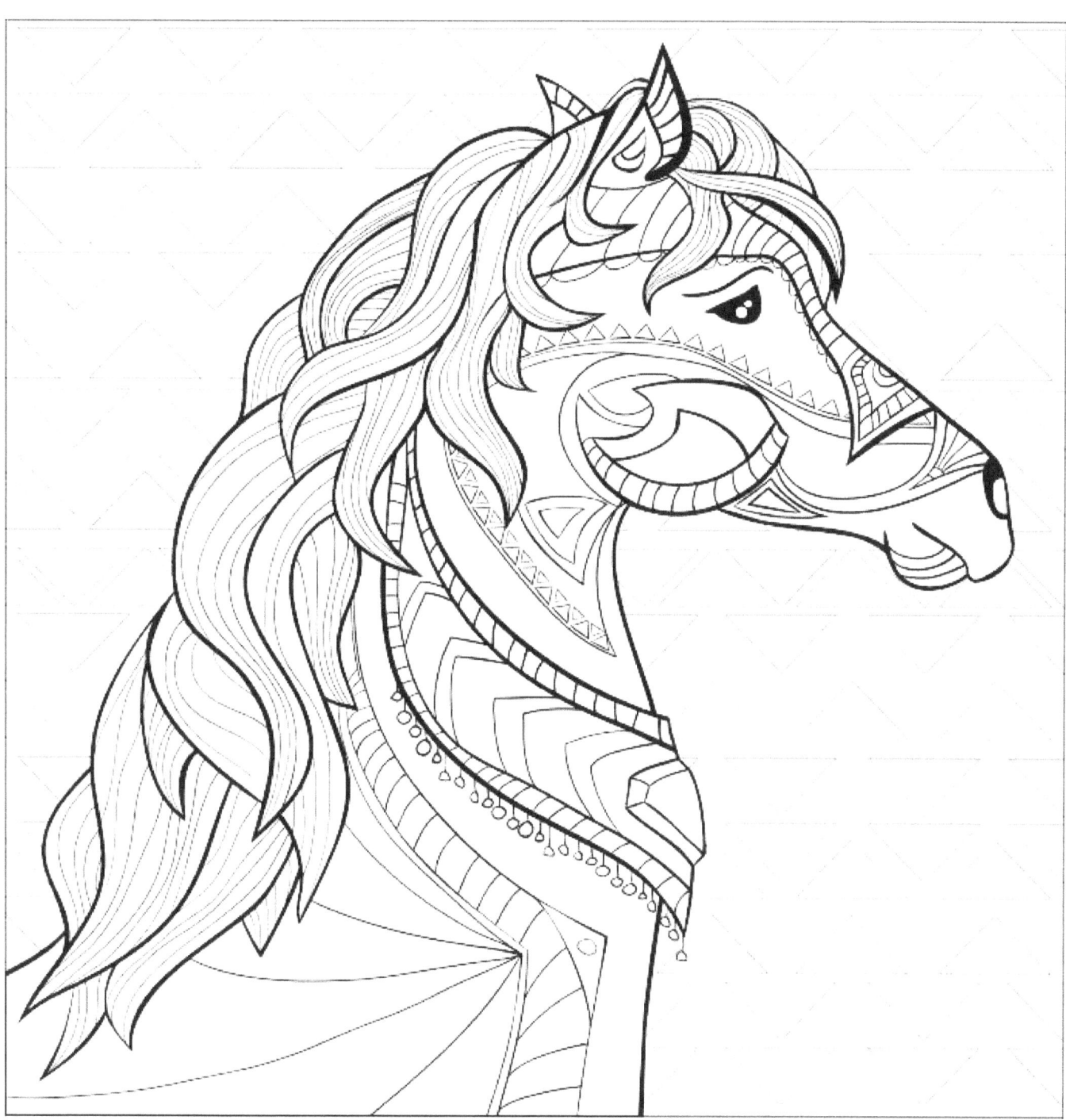

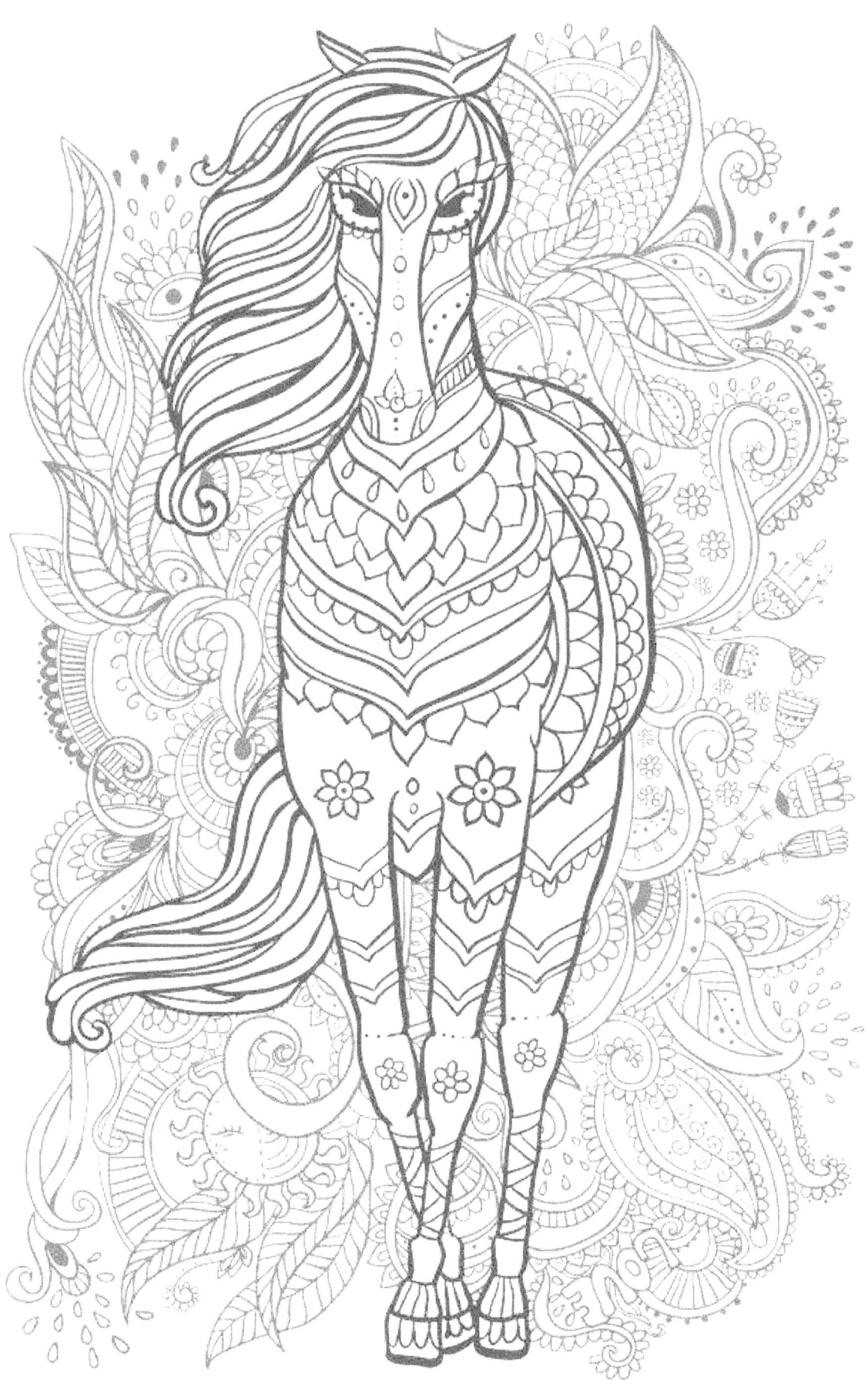

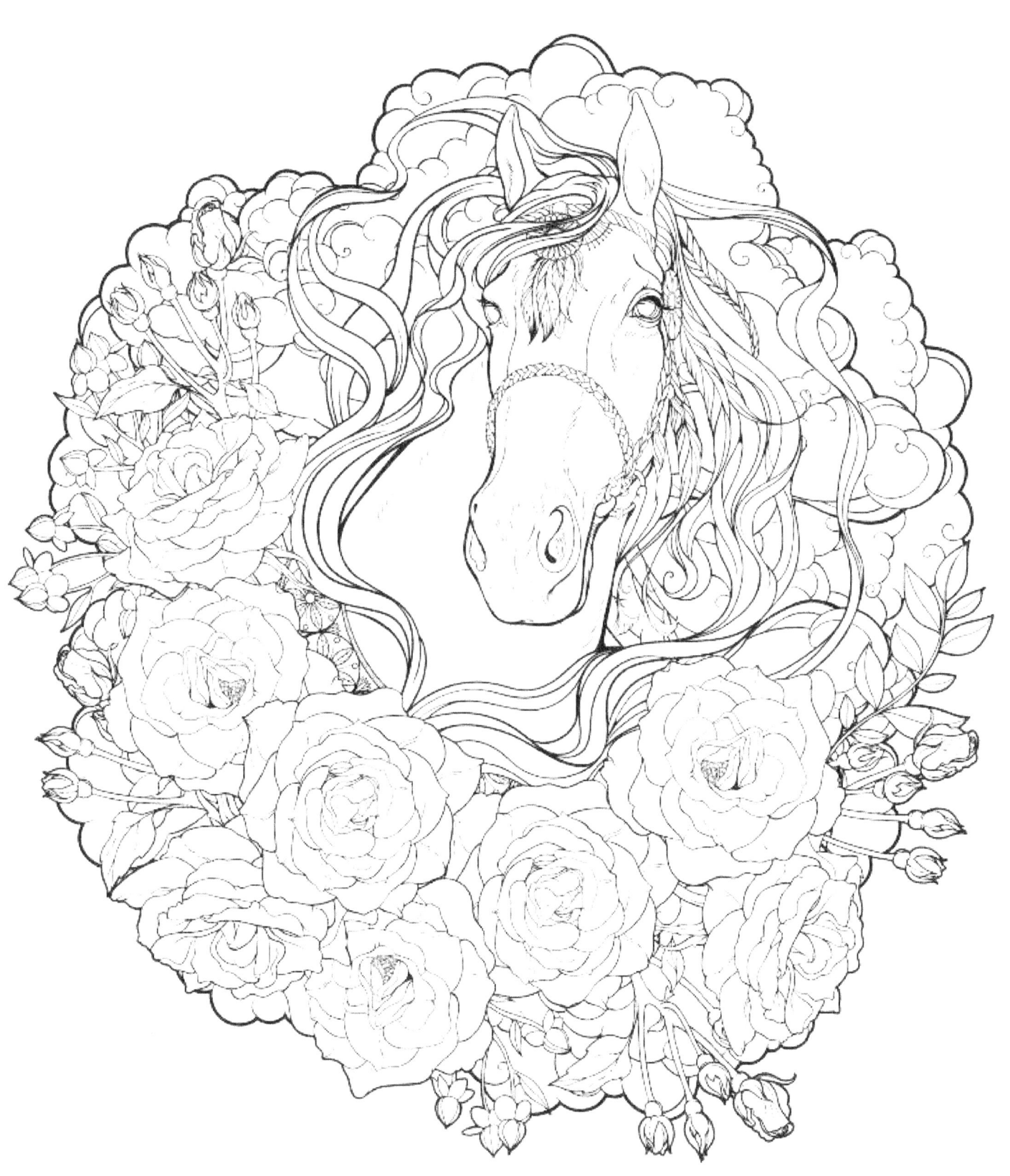

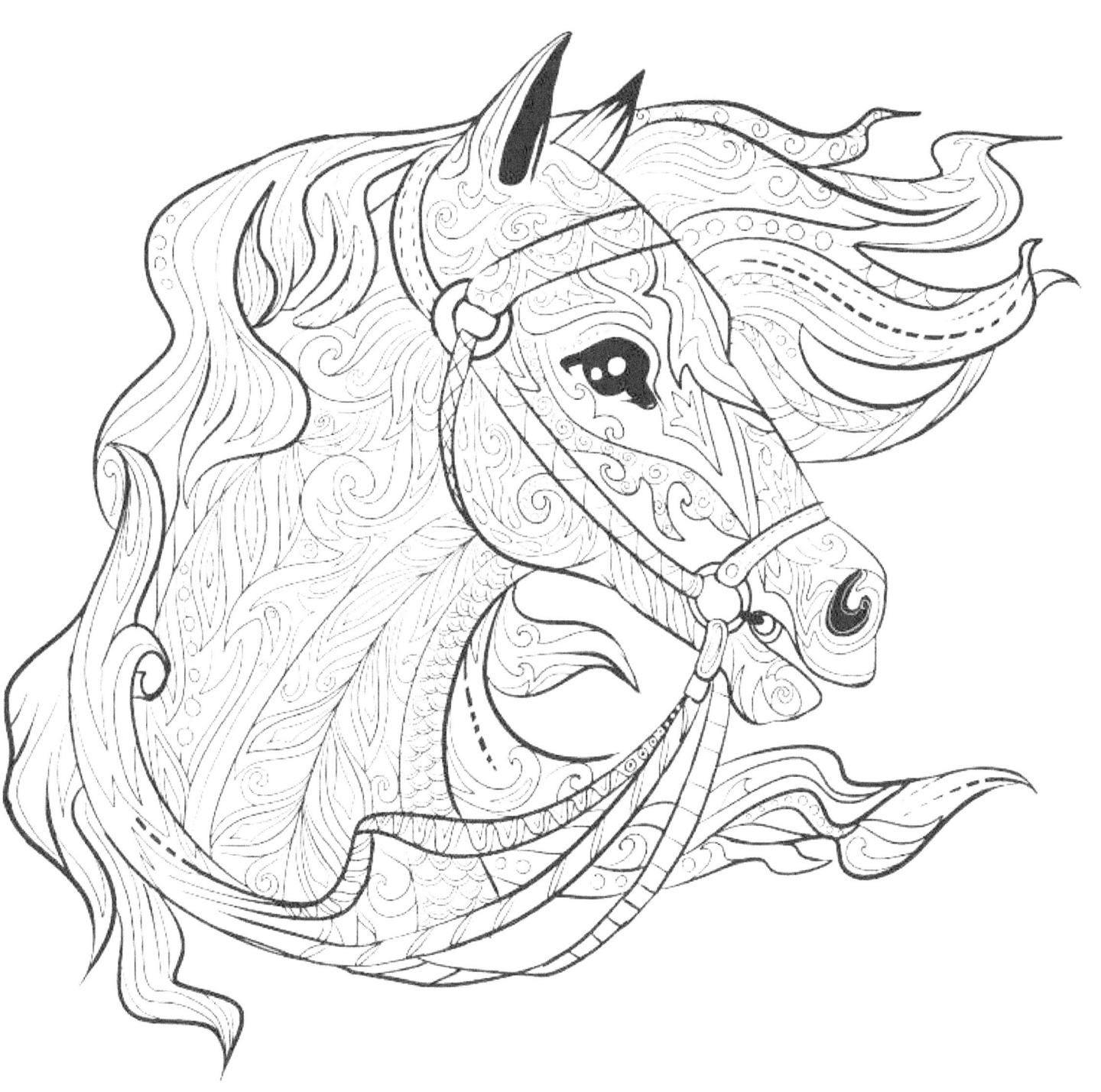

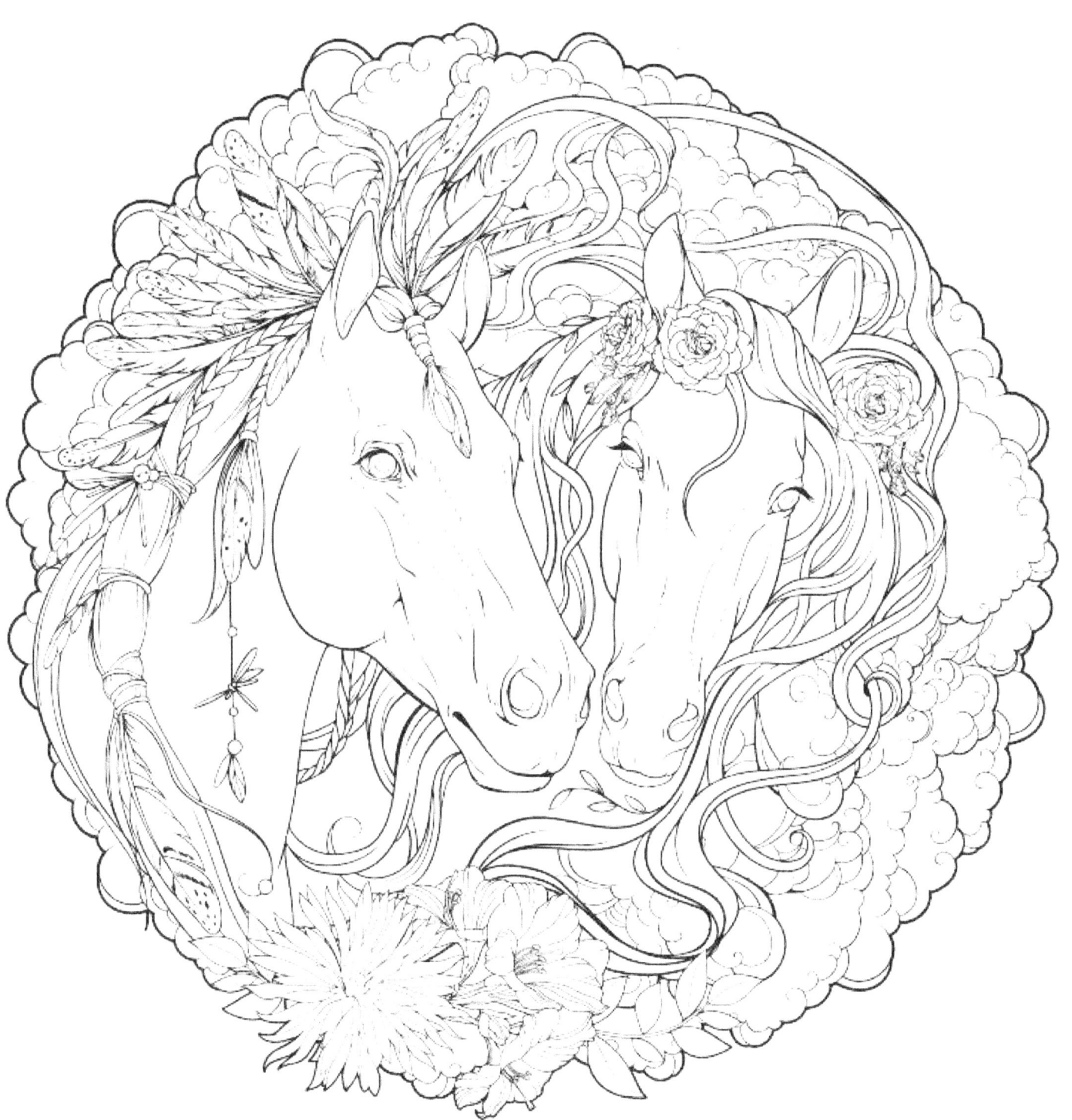